BOB WARDEN'S

Over 120 Quick and Hearty
Pressure Cooker Recipes

BOB WARDEN
WITH CHRISTIAN STELLA

QUAIL RIDGE PRESS
Preserving America's Food Heritage

Book design, food photographs, and illustrations by Christian and Elise Stella

Please read and adhere to all manufacturer's manuals
before operating any kitchen device.

Manufactured in the USA
ISBN 978-1-938879-06-7

Front cover: Perfect Pot Roast, page 37; Cream of Chicken Soup with Gnocchi Dumplings, page 33;
Minestrone Soup with Tortellini, page 15; Vanilla Bean Cheesecake, page 191
Back cover: Beef Burgundy, page 57; Most Excellent Macaroni and Cheese, page 171;
Cinnamon Apples with Granola and Ice Cream, page 195

QUAIL RIDGE PRESS
P. O. Box 123 • Brandon, MS 39043 • 1-800-343-1583
info@quailridge.com • www.quailridge.com

TABLE OF CONTENTS

THE MODERN PRESSURE COOKER

MY FASCINATION WITH PRESSURE cookers began at a young age, watching my mother wield several of the old-fashioned variety at the same time. She was constantly regulating the heat on the stove to keep each at its appropriate temperature.

She had it mastered. Thanksgivings were particularly showy, all cookers blazing, while I stood in awe, and the rest of the family stared like they were witnessing a woman on the edge.

Watching my mother in the kitchen on our farm in Iowa, I would have never guessed that one day I'd be equipping my own mass of pressure cookers in front of television cameras. Demonstrating something I'm truly passionate about. Moving from cooker to the cooker, releasing the pressure on one, and then the next. Cooking an entire feast all at once, just as my mother did so many years ago. But let's not sell her short.

Today's electronic cookers do all the work for you. They generate their own heat to minimize the scorching of a high heat stovetop; they heat to the appropriate temperature to build the exact amount of pressure at the touch of a button, and they have multiple safety features in place to keep the pressure in the cooker, and not all over your kitchen's ceiling.

I've written this book to share the favorite of my pressure cooker recipes. Recipes from the farm in Iowa while I was growing up, recipes I developed on air at QVC, and all the recipes in between. Like pressure cookers themselves, things have changed over the years. Ingredients are easier to come by than ever, available in more convenient forms that require less grunt work. By far, these are the fastest recipes for the heartiest family style dishes that I've ever compiled.

Most of all, I'd like to show that a pressure cooker is a truly versatile tool, capable of cooking more than just a pot roast. My mother knew it all those years ago with all those cookers on the stove. Then again, she did cook a darn good pot roast.

ELECTRONIC
PRESSURE COOKERS

T HE RECIPES IN THIS BOOK WERE specifically written, and tested on an electronic pressure cooker. If you own a stovetop, non-electric pressure cooker, turn to the next page for tips on making the recipes in this book.

Please refer to the instruction manual that came with your pressure cooker, reading and adhering to all warnings and precautions before attempting to make any recipes in this book! As there are many varieties of pressure cookers on the market, your manual should be your final source of guidance in using your particular make of pressure cooker.

Electronic pressure cookers are an all in one solution to pressure cooking that are extremely safe, energy efficient, and easy to operate. Much like a modern crock-pot or slow cooker (in fact many pressure cookers also include a slow cooker setting), electronic pressure cookers generate their own cooking heat, and do all of the cooking for you, based on internal gauges, and the settings that you input on the digital display.

Most cookers have two heat settings, HIGH and LOW, and the recipes in this book are written with that in mind. Your cooker may also have a medium setting, which you can disregard when following my recipes.

Some electronic pressure cookers forego the HIGH and LOW cook settings, and display the amount of cooking pressure using the term "PSI" or pounds per square inch. For these cookers, the recipes in this book that are listed to be cooked on "HIGH" can be cooked at 12–15psi, and the recipes to be cooked on "LOW" can be cooked at 5–8psi.

Other electronic pressure cookers use the term "kPa" to display cooking power. For these cookers, consider "HIGH" to be 80kPa, and "LOW" to be 40kPa.

The recipes in this book refer to two methods for releasing the pressure after cooking. A "quick release" involves releasing the pressure rapidly via your model of cooker's pressure release valve to stop the cooking. A "natural release" is when you simply let the cooker sit after cooking until the built up pressure dissipates on its own. For more on how to safely perform these specific actions, refer to the manual that came with your particular model.

Pressure Cookers

T HOUGH THE RECIPES IN THIS BOOK were specifically written for an electronic pressure cooker, if you own a stovetop, traditional pressure cooker, they can be made quite easily, and with very little adaptation.

Please refer to the instruction manual that came with your pressure cooker, reading, and adhering to all warnings and precautions before attempting to make any recipes in this book! As there are many varieties of pressure cookers on the market, your manual should be your final source of guidance in using your particular make of pressure cooker.

The recipes in this book use the terms "HIGH" and "LOW" as cooking temperatures, standard settings for an electronic cooker. Stovetop pressure cookers almost always calculate the temperature in "PSI" or pounds per square inch. For these stovetop cookers, the recipes in this book that are listed to be cooked on "HIGH" can be cooked at 15psi, and the recipes to be cooked on "LOW" can be cooked at 7½psi.

Once you've brought your stovetop cooker up to the proper psi, immediately lower the stove's heat to medium or as low as you need for your cooker to maintain that constant psi.

The recipes in this book refer to two methods for releasing the pressure after

cooking. A "quick release" involves releasing the pressure rapidly via your model of cooker's pressure release valve to stop the cooking. A "natural release" is when you simply let the cooker sit after cooking until the built up pressure dissipates on its own. Some stovetop cookers require you to run cold water over the lid to rapidly release the pressure, and perform what this book refers to as a "quick release." For more on how to safely perform these specific actions, refer to the manual that came with your particular model.

As many stovetop cookers are exposed to a harsher heat source (your stove) than the ones built into an electronic cooker, it is recommended that you place a heat diffuser between the stove, and the cooker when cooking beans, rice, pasta, or desserts to reduce food sticking, and possibly burning.

RELIEVING THE PRESSURE
OF PRESSURE COOKING ON A BUDGET

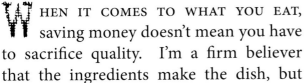

WHEN IT COMES TO WHAT YOU EAT, saving money doesn't mean you have to sacrifice quality. I'm a firm believer that the ingredients make the dish, but that doesn't mean I'm not thrifty! I am always looking for a better way, whether I'm tinkering with a new recipe or in the case of saving money… grocery shopping. Now with prices increasing, here are a few ways I've found to let the air out of a ballooning grocery bill.

Buy in bulk. Pressure cooking is perfect for bulk shopping. When you can cook an entire roast in under an hour, there's no reason to wait for special occasions to make one up. Not only are roasts usually cheaper than smaller cuts of meat, they're all but guaranteed to yield lunch money saving leftovers!

Shop the ads. I'll usually choose which recipes to cook for the week based on whether or not the ingredients are on sale. While most people look to sales on meats to make up their minds, I like to make recipes with at least two or three of the ingredients

on sale. With over 120 in this book, it's not as hard as it sounds!

Start an herb garden. Fresh herbs are very low maintenance plants, and you'll probably find that once they start growing, they just don't stop! A few packets of seeds for only a few dollars, and you'll be in the green. When they're growing too fast to use up, dry them in a food dehydrator, and give jars of dried herbs as gifts.

Buy inexpensive cuts of meat. I use my pressure cooker almost every day, but you'd never see me cooking a filet mignon in it! It's unnecessary, as inexpensive and ordinarily tough cuts of meat like round steak can cook to fork-tender in minutes.

Keep a well-stocked pantry. While it may seem expensive to overstock a pantry, it really does pay off over time. Last minute meals and snacks will be readily prepared, saving you from ordering out. Dried beans are a great source of protein when you don't have any meat in the fridge, and the pressure cooker can cook them up in no time.

Choosing the Best Cuts of Beef

With all of the pressure cooking that I do, sometimes I feel like the grocery store is my second home! A good grocery store with a great meat case is a thing of beauty, beckoning you to cook to your heart's content. That is, as long as you have an idea of what you're looking for.

While pressure cooking is an exciting, energy efficient, fast, and flavorful way to cook—it doesn't change one of the main fundamentals of cooking—to make good food, you're going to need good ingredients. What it may change, however, is your perception of just what is good.

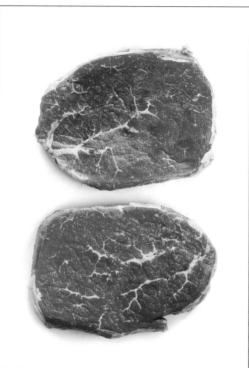

When shopping for beef, typically the most inexpensive cuts are also the toughest. With tons of connecting tissue for your teeth to chew, and very little fat marbled throughout them, they're certainly not butter knife tender, and have nothing to keep them moist. Round, chuck, and brisket roasts or steaks all fall into this category. Round steaks (pictured) look beautiful until you grill, broil, or skillet-fry them, take a bite, and realize that your creation is as tough as shoe leather. But these are good, healthier cuts of meat with less fat, and even more of a concentrated beef flavor than the more expensive, "tender" cuts of beef.

Typically, slow cooking tough cuts of beef for several hours is the best option, especially with roasts. This is where the pressure cooker really shines, producing the same, tender results in under an hour. Now, inexpensive roasts and tough cuts of meat literally fall apart in a realistic amount of time.

Keep in mind that chuck and round roasts are interchangeable, with the same cooking time for any recipe you use them in. This is good to know when one goes on sale or simply is not available. Though the pressure cooker does a great job of breaking up the tough connecting tissue of just about any cut of meat, chuck roasts have more fat than round, and will cook to be even more tender. It's up to you whether you prefer slightly more tender or slightly less fat. With all cuts of meat, I would highly suggest finding the most uniformly thick piece, for nice, and even cooking.

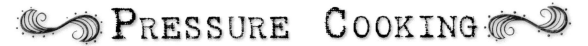

PRESSURE COOKING

PRODUCE

THOUGH A PRESSURE COOKER CAN DO a number on even the toughest cuts of meat, it is still a HIGHLY versatile piece of equipment entirely capable of cooking fresh and perfectly cooked fruits and vegetables.

The secrets to pressure cooked vegetables that aren't overcooked are lightning fast cooking times followed by a quick release of the pressure. In the case of more delicate vegetables, such as broccoli florets, the margin between perfectly cooked and completely overdone is as thin as 1 minute.

The firmer the vegetable, the better the results. Squash, with their thick rind cook particularly well, and you may find that the pressure cooker makes the best corn on the cob you've ever had.

A metal steamer basket, small enough to fit into the pressure cooker, will yield better results as it lifts the vegetables out of the liquid necessary to cook. Many companies sell them specifically for pressure cookers, and they're mostly interchangeable regardless of brand, as long as they're made for the same quart cooker. The easiest place

to find them is online, but an in-store fix can be had by purchasing a small metal colander instead.

Cooking a one-pot meal with meat and vegetables will almost always benefit from a two step cooking process. Refer to my cooking charts to find the cook time of your longest cooking vegetable, and then stop the cooking process short by that much time, releasing the pressure with a quick release. Then, add the vegetables, and cook for their recommended time. Release the pressure with a second quick release for the a perfectly cooked one-pot meal. While it may seem inconvenient, you can chop and prep the vegetables during the first step of cooking to save time!

Speaking of saving time, when you first remove the lid on a finished dish it is often so hot that a bag of frozen vegetables can be stirred right in, and completely cooked through residual heat. Take the bag out of the freezer, and leave on the counter as the dish is cooking to slightly thaw by the time the pressure cooker's lid comes off.

INDISPENSABLE
TIME SAVING TIPS

TIME IS OF THE ESSENCE! WHETHER you're always on the go or a hungry family is always at your heels, pressure cooking is here to save the minutes of the day. The following time saving tips can save you even more of those minutes; while it may seem that they're getting into the minutiae of cooking, for me, every second counts!

Arrange and prep your ingredients first. Grab all of your pantry items and spices before you start cooking to minimize back and forth trips. Measure and cut your ingredients at the same time, and following the cooking steps of a recipe will be as easy as 1 2 3.

Plan accordingly. Plan the entire meal and how you will prepare it in advance to utilize multiple cooking methods. Plan to make a salad while dinner is in the pressure cooker, or plan to have a pot of water heating on the stove for pasta as you prep the meat course ingredients for the pressure cooker. This way, everything will come out at the same time.

Cook a one-pot meal. It should go without saying that the pressure cooker

makes perfect one-pot meals, saving tons of time on cleanup.

Cut meat into smaller portions. Cutting a roast into two-inch thick pieces to cook under pressure can cut your cooking time in half.

Chop extra. If a recipe calls for half of a diced onion, dice the whole thing, and save the excess in a food storage bag or container in the fridge for use later in the week. Chopped onion is always good to have on hand. It freezes well, too, so why not chop a few?

Use frozen vegetables. With the pressure cooker, the cooking time of vegetables is not exactly an issue, but the cleaning and chopping time just may be. Cut time by letting the frozen food aisle cut things for you! Most stores also sell chopped fresh vegetables in the produce aisle now, and jarred minced garlic will have you asking who spends their time peeling garlic these days?

Use your pressure cooker's quick release valve! What are you waiting for? Letting the pressure release naturally is not always necessary.

PANTRY

SHOPPING LIST

Being prepared from the start can save you a ton of time, both at home and in the grocery store. The following lists include the ingredients used most throughout the recipes in this book. I would suggest filling the gaps in your spice cabinet first.

SPICES

bay leaves
cayenne pepper
celery salt
chili powder
cinnamon
cumin
garlic powder
Italian seasoning
mustard powder
nutmeg
onion powder
oregano
paprika
parsley flakes
poultry seasoning
rosemary
tarragon
thyme
white pepper

DRY GOODS

beef base
chicken base
diced tomatoes, canned
Dijon mustard
flour
ketchup
lemon juice
light brown sugar
minced garlic
olive oil
red wine
sugar
tomato paste
vanilla extract
vegetable broth
vegetable oil
white wine
worcestershire sauce
yellow mustard

PERISHABLES

bell peppers
butter
carrots
celery
cream cheese
eggs
lemons
milk
onions
Parmesan cheese
redskin potatoes
sour cream

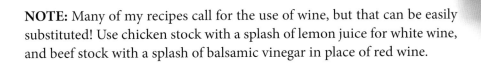

NOTE: Many of my recipes call for the use of wine, but that can be easily substituted! Use chicken stock with a splash of lemon juice for white wine, and beef stock with a splash of balsamic vinegar in place of red wine.

BIG FLAVOR IN A SMALL PACKAGE

ALL FOODS COOKED IN A PRESSURE cooker require at least ½ cup of liquid to create the steam necessary to bring the cooker up to pressure. In most cases, pressure cooking in water would be a waste of a layer of flavor that you can add to the final dish. When it comes to good cooking in general, layering flavors is key. That's where a good stock or broth comes in.

Making fresh stocks is a time-consuming process that few people actually undertake, and cans or cartons of chicken, beef, vegetable, and other stocks or broths are extremely lacking in the flavor department. Bouillon cubes are so salty that the only thing I'd do with them is paint numbers on them and play Yahtzee. So what is there to use?

Bases. Bases are a high quality, highly concentrated paste that dissolves into a broth when added to water. The small five-inch tall jars are available in a wide variety of flavors, near the canned broths in just about any grocery store. The most readily available brand is called *Better than Bouillon*. While the jars usually cost around five dollars each, they make almost forty cups of broth, which would cost over twenty dollars canned. Quite simply, bases are the cheapest, and lightest way to carry home ten quarts of a good quality broth.

Bases come in all sorts of flavors, from chicken, and beef, to vegetable, mushroom, and even ham! While writing this book, I visited a dozen grocery stores, and they all carried chicken and beef base, but only two carried the full gamut of flavors. For this reason, I have only included chicken and beef in this book. I highly recommend picking up a jar of vegetable base if you see it, and substituting it (mixed with water) for the vegetable broth listed in my recipes.

Bases are not only made from real chicken, beef, or vegetables, they are the perfect choice for preparing recipes because you only make what you need.

Most **bases are turned into broth by mixing 1 teaspoon with 1 cup of water**, though they allow the flexibility of adjusting that amount to your taste. I like to add a small amount extra when cooking with a lot of water-releasing vegetables, such as onions or mushrooms.

The jars must be refrigerated after opening but last for up to a year.

SOUPS

Minestrone Soup with Tortellini	15
Ground Beef Chili	16
Chicken and Sausage Gumbo	17
Cabbage Soup with Polish Sausage	19
Butternut Squash Soup	20
Southern Seafood Gumbo	21
Cooled Cucumber and Coconut Soup	23
Spinach and Lentil Soup	24
Crab and Corn Bisque	25
Cinnamon Spiced Turkey Chili	27
Black Bean Soup	29
Split Pea and Bacon Soup	30
Brunswick Stew	31
Cream of Chicken Soup with Gnocchi Dumplings	33

SOUPS

MINESTRONE SOUP WITH TORTELLINI

LOOSELY TRANSLATED FROM ITALIAN, Minestrone means "The Big Soup" for a reason. Though its ingredients have never been set in stone, one thing has—it's fit to be a full meal. This take is certainly no different with spoon after spoon of plump cheese stuffed tortellini; your family won't believe it went from fridge to table in only 20 minutes.

1. ADD oil to pressure cooker, and heat on HIGH or "BROWN" with the lid off. Sauté onions, celery, carrots, and garlic until onions begin to sweat.

2. ADD remaining ingredients, and stir. Securely lock on cooker's lid, set cooker to HIGH, and cook 5 minutes.

3. PERFORM a quick release to release cooker's pressure. Safely remove lid, and check tortellini for doneness. If it is too al dente for your likeness continue to boil on HIGH or "BROWN" with the lid off, until it is where you want it. Serve topped with Parmesan cheese.

SHOPPING LIST

2 tablespoons olive oil

1 white onion, chopped small

2 stalks celery, sliced ¼-inch thick

2 carrots, sliced ¼-inch thick

1 tablespoon minced garlic

1 (8-ounce) package cheese tortellini (available in dry goods pasta aisle)

4 cups vegetable broth

1 jar spaghetti sauce

1 (14-ounce) can diced tomatoes

1½ teaspoons Italian seasoning

1 teaspoon sugar

¼ teaspoon ground black pepper

Shredded Parmesan cheese, for garnish

Bob's Tips

These days there are plenty of varieties of jarred spaghetti sauces and dried tortellini to choose from, so why not try making this recipe with a jar of chunky mushroom tomato sauce or spinach tortellini, or both?

GROUND BEEF CHILI

MAKE SURE YOU HAVE PLENTY OF CRACKERS on hand when preparing this wintertime classic. My legume-free recipe is a terrific base to add a can or two of whichever beans you have in the pantry.

1. ADD vegetable oil to pressure cooker, and heat on HIGH or "BROWN" with the lid off, until sizzling. Add ground beef, breaking it up with a spoon or spatula as it browns.

2. ONCE beef is browning well, add onion and garlic, and stir in for 2 minutes.

3. ADD remaining ingredients, except Cheddar cheese, and stir. Securely lock on cooker's lid, set cooker to HIGH, and cook 8 minutes.

4. LET pressure release naturally 10 minutes before quick releasing remaining pressure and safely removing the lid. Salt and pepper to taste, and serve topped with shredded Cheddar cheese.

SHOPPING LIST

1 tablespoon vegetable oil

2 pounds lean ground beef

1 cup chopped onion

1 tablespoon minced garlic

1 (14- to 16-ounce) can diced tomatoes, with liquid

2 teaspoons chicken base (see page: 12) mixed into 2 cups water

1 (4-ounce) can mild green chile peppers, with liquid

1 teaspoon sugar

½ teaspoon cumin

2 teaspoons chili powder

2 tablespoons cornmeal

Salt and pepper to taste

Shredded Cheddar cheese, for garnish

Bob's Tips

Chili is a prime dish for all sorts of wonderful toppings. Shredded Cheddar cheese goes without saying, but how about spicy pepper jack cheese? Sour cream, plain yogurt, or even avocado can cool things down a bit. Chopped onions or even green onion tops can add a little flavor and crunch.

CHICKEN AND SAUSAGE GUMBO

TYPICALLY SERVED OVER RICE, THIS ONE pot Louisiana gumbo is cooked all at once in only six minutes! This hearty, Creole stew gets its name, Gumbo, from an African word for okra, and for good reason, as okra is pulling double duty here by actually thickening the soup as it cooks!

1. ADD butter, garlic, sausage, onion, bell pepper, and celery to cooker, and cook on HIGH or "BROWN" with the lid off, until sausage begins to brown and vegetables begin to sweat.

2. COAT chicken with flour before adding to cooker.

3. ADD remaining ingredients, and stir. Securely lock on the lid, set cooker to HIGH, and cook 6 minutes.

4. LET pressure release naturally 10 minutes before quick releasing remaining pressure and safely removing the lid. Season to taste before serving.

 If you aren't a fan of spicy foods, you may omit the ground red pepper; and if you are a fan of spicy foods, you'll definitely want to bring a bottle of Louisiana hot sauce or Tabasco to the table.

SHOPPING LIST

2 tablespoons butter

1 tablespoon minced garlic

½ pound andouille or smoked sausage, cut into ¼-inch slices

1 cup chopped onion

1 green bell pepper, chopped large

2 stalks celery, cut into ¼-inch slices

1 pound boneless, skinless chicken thighs, each thigh cut into 3 strips

3 tablespoons flour

1½ cups frozen sliced okra

1 cup white rice, uncooked

4 teaspoons chicken base (see page: 12) mixed into 4 cups water

1 (14- to 16-ounce) can diced tomatoes

2 bay leaves

1 tablespoon parsley flakes

1 teaspoon onion powder

½ teaspoon paprika

½ teaspoon ground red or cayenne pepper

Salt and pepper to taste

CABBAGE SOUP WITH POLISH SAUSAGE

If it's possible for a soup to be both hearty and light at the same time, this is the one. The combination of the chunky potatoes, sausage, and loads of cabbage with such a light and refreshing broth is a sure-fire success for any dinner with guests!

1. ADD butter to pressure cooker, and heat on HIGH or "BROWN" with the lid off. Sauté onions, and garlic in butter until onions begin to brown.

2. ADD remaining ingredients, and stir. Securely lock on cooker's lid, set cooker to HIGH, and cook 4 minutes.

3. PERFORM a quick release to release cooker's pressure. Safely remove lid, and serve.

This soup goes great with a nice rye bread. For a creamier broth, mix ¼ cup half-and-half into the pot just before serving, or try garnishing with a dollop of sour cream.

SHOPPING LIST

2 tablespoons butter or margarine

1 white onion, sliced into ⅙-inch rings

1½ teaspoons minced garlic

4 cups sliced cabbage (may use coleslaw shreds, sold in bagged lettuce section)

2 cups red potatoes, cut in ½-inch cubes with skin on

8 ounces smoked kielbasa sausage, sliced into thick discs, then cubed

2 teaspoons chicken base (see page: 12) mixed into 2 cups water

2 cups vegetable broth

1 tablespoon white vinegar

1 tablespoon dried parsley

1 bay leaf

1 teaspoon celery salt

1 teaspoon sugar

¼ teaspoon ground black pepper

BUTTERNUT SQUASH SOUP

THIS TASTY SOUP HAS BECOME A STAPLE for my family at Thanksgiving. We get a big pot started first thing in the morning, and use it to not only kick start the wonderful smells in the house, but to stave off appetites that can't quite wait until the big meal.

1. HEAT olive oil, garlic, and onion in pressure cooker on HIGH or "BROWN" with lid off, until onions are sizzling and begin to sweat.

2. COVER with remaining ingredients, except half-and-half. Securely lock on cooker's lid, set cooker to HIGH, and cook 8 minutes.

3. PERFORM a quick release to release cooker's pressure. Safely remove lid, and, using a slotted spoon, transfer squash chunks to a food processor or blender. Add half-and-half, and blend until smooth.

4. REINTRODUCE blended squash mixture to the cooking pot, mixing with cooking liquid until combined well. Serve hot. If soup has cooled, heat on HIGH or "BROWN" with lid off, until hot.

SHOPPING LIST

1 tablespoon olive oil

2 teaspoons minced garlic

½ onion, diced

2 medium-size butternut squash, peeled, seeded, and cut into 2-inch chunks

3 teaspoons chicken base (see page: 12) mixed into 3 cups water

½ teaspoon ground sage

⅛ teaspoon nutmeg

¼ cup half-and-half

Salt and pepper to taste

Bob's Tips

If squash is too thick to blend smoothly, add a ladle or two of the cooking liquid until there is enough liquid to blend. Try serving with a dollop of plain yogurt to make the soup even creamier.

SOUTHERN SEAFOOD GUMBO

A GOOD SEAFOOD GUMBO IS LIKE A Who's Who of everything delicious in the ocean. Serve it in large bowls, leaving plenty of room to stir in some white rice. Make up some hush puppies to go with it, and you are one spoonful away from utter contentment.

1. ADD all ingredients to cooker, and stir. Securely lock on cooker's lid, set cooker to HIGH, and cook 3 minutes.

2. PERFORM a quick release to release cooker's pressure, and safely remove lid. Salt and pepper to taste before serving as is or over rice.

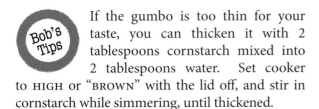

If the gumbo is too thin for your taste, you can thicken it with 2 tablespoons cornstarch mixed into 2 tablespoons water. Set cooker to HIGH or "BROWN" with the lid off, and stir in cornstarch while simmering, until thickened.

SHOPPING LIST

1 pound white fish fillets (cod, haddock, etc.) cut into 1-inch pieces

1 pound shrimp, peeled and deveined

½ pound lump crabmeat, optional

2 tablespoons butter or margarine

1 tablespoon minced garlic

1 onion, chopped

1 red bell pepper, chopped

2 stalks celery, cut into ¼-inch slices

1½ cups frozen sliced okra

3 teaspoons chicken base (see page: 12) mixed into 3 cups water

1 (14- to 16-ounce) can diced tomatoes

2 bay leaves

1 teaspoon onion powder

1 tablespoon Old Bay Seasoning

½ teaspoon ground red or cayenne pepper

Salt and pepper to taste

10 MINS   1 MINS   SIX   HIGH

COOLED CUCUMBER AND COCONUT SOUP

A COLD SOUP MAY BE THE LAST THING you'd expect to cook in a pressure cooker! This soup could be made without cooking at all, but cooking it for 1 minute under pressure brings out all sorts of wonderful flavors, and then locks them in for a refreshing dish on a hot summer day.

1. RESERVE 1 cucumber for garnish. Peel remaining 2 cucumbers, and slice in half lengthwise. Spoon out seeds, and discard. Roughly chop peeled and cleaned cucumber halves.

2. HEAT olive oil, garlic, and onion in pressure cooker on HIGH or "BROWN" with the lid off, until onions are sizzling and begin to sweat.

3. ADD remaining ingredients, except coconut milk and toasted coconut. Securely lock on cooker's lid, set cooker to HIGH, and cook 1 minute.

SHOPPING LIST

3 medium-size cucumbers, divided

1 tablespoon olive oil

1 teaspoon minced garlic

½ onion, diced

1 cup vegetable broth

1 tablespoon lime juice

½ teaspoon salt

¼ teaspoon ground black pepper

2 teaspoons sugar

1 (14- to 16-ounce) can unsweetened coconut milk

Toasted shredded coconut, for garnish

4. PERFORM a quick release to release cooker's pressure. Safely remove lid, and stir in coconut milk. Cover, and refrigerate until cold, about 2 hours.

5. BLEND cold soup in a blender or food processor until smooth. Serve topped with thinly sliced cucumber and toasted coconut.

Bob's Tips

To toast shredded coconut: preheat oven to 350°, and spread coconut on a sheet pan in a thin layer. Bake 6–8 minutes, shaking sheet pan halfway through to stir around.

SOUPS

SPINACH AND LENTIL SOUP

THIS REFRESHING SOUP'S LIGHT FLAVORS are delicious but not overpowering. One of the great things about pressure cooking is that it makes lentils an everyday ingredient, no longer too time consuming to prepare. Quite simply, they're one of the most balanced foods on the planet, loaded with protein, fiber, and even iron!

1. RINSE lentils in a colander, picking through them to make sure there are no stones or other objects.

2. ADD all ingredients to cooker, except spinach, and stir. Securely lock on cooker's lid, set cooker to HIGH, and cook 8 minutes.

3. PERFORM a quick release to release cooker's pressure, and safely remove the lid. Stir in thawed spinach and salt and pepper to taste. Serve immediately.

SHOPPING LIST

1 cup dried lentils

2 stalks celery, chopped

2 carrots, peeled and chopped

2 tablespoons olive oil

1 tablespoon minced garlic

4 teaspoons chicken base (see page: 12) mixed into 4 cups water

2 cups vegetable broth

2 tablespoons lemon juice

1 teaspoon lemon zest

1 teaspoon cumin

1 bay leaf

1 (12-ounce) bag frozen chopped spinach, thawed

Salt and pepper to taste

Bob's Tips
You can add chicken to this soup by cutting 1 pound of chicken tenders into 1-inch long chunks, and adding them to cooker before cooking under pressure. No need to adjust the cooking time!

CRAB AND CORN BISQUE

BISQUE IS MORE THAN JUST A FANCY NAME for soup. It describes this thick, creamy, steaming goodness you can achieve in your very own kitchen, no French chefs required.

1. HEAT butter in pressure cooker on HIGH or "BROWN" with the lid off, until melted.

2. ADD onion and carrots, and sauté 2–3 minutes, until onions begin to turn translucent.

3. COVER with remaining ingredients, except cream-style corn, heavy cream, and garnish. Securely lock on cooker's lid, set cooker to HIGH, and cook 4 minutes.

4. PERFORM a quick release to release cooker's pressure. Safely remove the lid, and use a slotted spoon to spoon out and transfer onions, carrots, and crabmeat to a blender or food processor. Blend until smooth.

SHOPPING LIST

4 tablespoons butter or margarine

1 onion, diced

4 carrots, peeled and sliced into ⅛-inch discs

2 teaspoons chicken base (see page: 12) mixed into 2 cups water

½ pound lump crabmeat

1 tablespoon lemon juice

¼ cup dry sherry

½ teaspoon paprika

1 (14- to 16-ounce) can cream-style corn

½ cup heavy cream (may use half-and-half)

Salt and pepper to taste

Additional lump crabmeat, for garnish

5. RETURN onion, carrot, and crab mixture to pot. Stir in cream-style corn and heavy cream. If bisque cools down too much, set cooker to HIGH or "BROWN" with the lid off to bring it back up to a simmer. Salt and pepper to taste, and serve topped with a spoonful of lump crabmeat.

Use fresh crab if possible, and prepare yourself for a luscious treat. Replace chicken base with 2 cups water, and cook crab, in the shell, while following the rest of the recipe. Remove crabmeat from shells before blending in step 4.

10 MINS   15 MINS   SIX   LOW

CINNAMON SPICED TURKEY CHILI

THIS TURKEY CHILI IS A WINTER FAVORITE of mine for those snow-covered days when a cup of spiced cider just isn't enough. The earthy aroma and complex flavors work so well, you'd never even know it was pretty good for you, too!

1. ADD vegetable oil to pressure cooker, and heat on HIGH or "BROWN" with the lid off. Add ground turkey, breaking it up with a wooden spoon as it browns.

2. ONCE turkey is browning well, add onion and garlic, and cook 3 additional minutes. Drain off half of the liquid in cooker.

3. ADD remaining ingredients, and stir. Securely lock on cooker's lid, set cooker to LOW, and cook 15 minutes.

4. LET pressure release naturally 10 minutes before quick releasing remaining pressure. Safely remove lid, and serve with a dollop of sour cream.

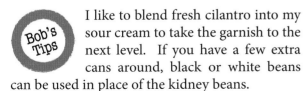 I like to blend fresh cilantro into my sour cream to take the garnish to the next level. If you have a few extra cans around, black or white beans can be used in place of the kidney beans.

SHOPPING LIST

1 tablespoon vegetable oil

2 pounds ground turkey

1 onion, chopped large

1 tablespoon minced garlic

2 red bell peppers, chopped large

1 (15-ounce) can diced tomatoes, with liquid

1 (14-ounce) can red kidney beans, with liquid

1½ teaspoons chicken base (see page: 12) mixed into 1½ cups water

1 (6-ounce) can tomato paste

2 teaspoons celery salt

2 teaspoons sugar

1 teaspoon cumin

2 tablespoons cornmeal

1 teaspoon ground cinnamon

1 teaspoon coriander

1 teaspoon chili powder

¼ teaspoon ground black pepper

Sour cream, for garnish

PREP TIME	COOK TIME	SERVES	TEMPERATURE
10 MINS	35 MINS	SIX	HIGH

BLACK BEAN SOUP

THE CILANTRO REALLY TAKES THIS SOUP to the next level. Add cumin, chili powder, and lime juice, and you're eating black beans as you'll swear they were always meant to be.

1. HEAT oil, garlic, celery, onion, and bell pepper in pressure cooker on HIGH or "BROWN" with lid off for about 7 minutes, stirring frequently, until onions are translucent.

2. ADD black beans to cooker, and top with remaining ingredients, except sour cream. Securely lock on cooker's lid, set cooker to HIGH, and cook 35 minutes.

3. LET pressure release naturally 15 minutes, quick release remaining pressure, and safely remove lid.

4. MASH beans against the bottom and walls of cooker until ⅔ of the beans are broken up, thickening the soup.

5. SALT and pepper to taste, and serve topped with sour cream.

SHOPPING LIST

2 tablespoons vegetable oil

1 tablespoon minced garlic

1 stalk celery, chopped small

1 yellow onion, diced

1 red bell pepper, chopped

1 pound dried black beans, rinsed

4 teaspoons beef base (see page: 12) mixed into 4 cups water

1 cup water

2 tablespoons lime juice

1 bay leaf

1 tablespoon fresh cilantro, chopped

1 teaspoon cumin

1 teaspoon chili powder

1 tablespoon light brown sugar

Salt and pepper to taste

Sour cream, for garnish

Bob's Tips If you can find one, pick up an old-fashioned, red plastic ketchup squirt bottle (that you used to see at picnics, and that you fill yourself) to fill with the sour cream garnish. This will allow you to make designs on the top of the soup as seen in the picture at left.

SPLIT PEA AND BACON SOUP

JUST AS IT WORKS ITS MAGIC ON GREEN beans, the salty and hickory-smoked taste of bacon brings out a wonderful sweetness in this split pea soup. So split a loaf of crusty bread, and take this recipe for a dip.

1. ADD all ingredients to cooker, and fill with enough water to cover everything by 1½ inches. Stir well, until chicken base has dissolved. Securely lock on cooker's lid, set cooker to HIGH, and cook 10 minutes.

2. LET pressure release naturally 10 minutes before performing a quick release to release remaining pressure. Safely remove lid, and use a slotted spoon to scoop out 1 cup cooked split peas.

SHOPPING LIST

2 tablespoons butter or margarine

1 tablespoon minced garlic

1 onion, diced

2 carrots, peeled and diced

1 pound dried split peas

1 cup cooked bacon pieces (sold precooked in salad dressing aisle)

3 teaspoons chicken base (see page: 12)

1 bay leaf

3. BLEND the cup of split peas in blender or food processor, until smooth, adding liquid if too thick.

4. REINTRODUCE blended peas to cooking pot, mixing until well combined. Serve immediately.

Bob's Tips

Try adding 1 cup of frozen green peas after the initial cooking has finished, stirring in, and letting them sit for 2 minutes to heat through. You'll get all the flavors of traditional split pea soup with the crisp, sweet, and fresh crunch of green peas.

BRUNSWICK STEW

I WON'T ASK YOU TO BE COMPLETELY authentic, and use rabbit meat in this stew, chicken and ham work just fine. With heaps of meat, lima beans, and corn, if you don't have more meat and vegetables than broth, you don't have Brunswick stew!

1. ADD butter, ham, garlic, onion, and bell pepper to pressure cooker, and cook on HIGH or "BROWN" with the lid off, until ham begins to brown, and onions are translucent.

2. COAT chicken leg quarters with flour on all sides before adding to cooker.

3. ADD remaining ingredients, except lima beans and corn. Securely lock on cooker's lid, set cooker to HIGH, and cook 14 minutes.

4. LET pressure release naturally 10 minutes before quick releasing remaining pressure and safely removing the lid. Remove chicken legs, and set aside to cool 5 minutes.

SHOPPING LIST

2 tablespoons butter

½ pound smoked (country) ham, diced

1 tablespoon minced garlic

1 onion, chopped large

1 green bell pepper, chopped large

2 pounds chicken leg quarters

1 cup flour, to dredge chicken

2 cans diced tomatoes (14–16 ounces each)

3 teaspoons chicken base (see page: 12) mixed into 3 cups water

2 bay leaves

1½ cups lima beans, frozen

1½ cups corn kernels, frozen

Salt and pepper to taste

5. SET cooker to HIGH or "BROWN" with the lid off, and stir lima beans and corn into stew.

6. SHRED chicken meat off the bone using two forks. Discard bones, and return meat to the stew. Salt and pepper to taste before serving.

Many variations of Brunswick Stew are made with smoked meat for a really downhome taste. This is easily replicated by adding a teaspoon or two of liquid smoke before cooking!

CREAM OF CHICKEN SOUP WITH GNOCCHI DUMPLINGS

THIS CREAM OF CHICKEN SOUP RECIPE takes a totally original and delicious turn with the addition of Italian gnocchi dumplings. Now available in almost every grocery store's dry pasta aisle, gnocchi are small potato dumplings that cook up as large and satisfying as a traditional dumpling without all the work!

1. HEAT butter in pressure cooker on HIGH or "BROWN," until melted.

2. COAT cubed chicken with flour on all sides before adding to cooker with celery. Sauté 2–3 minutes, until chicken is lightly browned.

3. COVER with remaining ingredients, except heavy cream.

4. SECURELY lock on cooker's lid, set cooker to HIGH, and cook 6 minutes.

5. PERFORM a quick release to release cooker's pressure. Safely remove lid, and slowly stir in heavy cream. Salt and pepper to taste, and serve immediately.

SHOPPING LIST

3 tablespoons butter or margarine

1 pound chicken tenders, cubed

3 tablespoons flour

2 stalks celery, diced small

4 teaspoons chicken base (see page: 12) mixed into 4 cups water

16 ounces dry gnocchi dumplings (sold in pasta aisle)

1 sprig fresh thyme or 1 teaspoon dried

1 bay leaf

1 teaspoon onion powder

1 tablespoon parsley flakes

¾ cup heavy cream (may use half-and-half)

Salt and pepper to taste

For firmer, more pasta-like gnocchi, add them with the heavy cream after the pressure cooking process. Switch the cooker to HIGH or "BROWN" with the lid off, and boil 3–4 minutes, until gnocchi begin to float.

Cooking Times
Beef

When cooking beef, browning the meat first will add more flavor, especially to the gravy. Letting the pressure release naturally for at least 10 minutes is recommended unless cooking thin cuts of meat.

Beef	Size	Liquid	Cook Minutes	Temp
Brisket	2–3 pounds	to cover	45	HIGH
Brisket	4–5 pounds	to cover	70	HIGH
Chuck Roast	3–4 pounds	2 cups	60	HIGH
Corned Beef	2–3 pounds	to cover	45	HIGH
Corned Beef	4–5 pounds	to cover	70	HIGH
Flank Steak	2–3 pounds	1 cup	35	HIGH
Ground Beef	1–2 pounds	1 cup	6	HIGH
Oxtails	any	to cover	45	HIGH
Rib Roast	3–4 pounds	2 cups	60	HIGH
Round Roast	3–4 pounds	2 cups	60	HIGH
Shanks	2-inch thick	1½ cups	45	HIGH
Short Ribs	any	1½ cups	30	HIGH
Shoulder Roast	3–4 pounds	2 cups	60	HIGH
Stew Meat	1-inch cubes	1 cup	20	HIGH
Thin Steaks	less than 1-inch	⅔ cup	15	HIGH

BEEF

Prep Time	Cook Time			Serves	Temperature
15 MINS	45 MINS			SIX	HIGH

BEEF

PERFECT POT ROAST

Quite simply, this is the easiest way to prepare a pot roast without sacrificing a lick of flavor. Fork-tender in an amazingly quick 45 minute cooking time!

1. ADD oil to pressure cooker, and heat on HIGH or "BROWN" with the lid off. Sprinkle roast with celery salt, onion powder, and ground black pepper.

2. PLACE roast in pressure cooker to brown. Flip, and brown other side.

3. POUR in wine, stab roast with a meat fork, and push the meat around the bottom of pan to release the glaze you've created.

4. ADD beef base mixture, garlic, thyme, bay leaves, and salt. Securely lock on cooker's lid, set cooker to HIGH, and cook 40 minutes.

5. PERFORM a quick release to release cooker's pressure. Safely remove lid, and add Vegetables. Re-lock pressure cooker's lid, set cooker to HIGH, and cook 5 minutes.

6. PERFORM a quick release to release the cooker's pressure. Serve covered in the au jus from cooker.

SHOPPING LIST

ROAST

4 tablespoons vegetable oil

1 (2- to 3-pound) beef chuck roast

½ teaspoon celery salt

½ teaspoon onion powder

Ground black pepper to taste

½ cup red wine

2 teaspoons beef base (see page: 12) mixed into 2 cups water

2 tablespoons minced garlic

1 sprig fresh thyme, or 1 teaspoon dried

2 bay leaves

1 teaspoon salt

VEGETABLES

6 small redskin potatoes, halved

2 small onions, peeled, and quartered

2 cups baby carrots

2 stalks celery, cut into 1-inch pieces

Bob's Tips

To thicken juices into gravy: combine 2 tablespoons cornstarch with 2 tablespoons water in a small dish; stir into cooker on HIGH or "BROWN" with the lid off, until thick. Pot roast can be prepared in advance, and refrigerated in an airtight container for up to five days.

BEEF

GROUND BEEF STROGANOFF

WHILE TRADITIONALLY MADE WITH STRIPS or cubes of beef, I've been making a ground beef variation of stroganoff for as long as I can remember. It's just one of those hearty family classics that reminds you why it's always a good idea to keep a pound of ground beef on hand.

1. ADD butter to pressure cooker, and heat on HIGH or "BROWN" with the lid off, until sizzling. Add ground beef, breaking it up with spoon or spatula as it browns.

2. ONCE ground beef is breaking up well, carefully drain most of the fat from the pot, then add onion and celery. Stir for 2 minutes, until onions start to turn translucent.

3. ADD remaining ingredients, except sour cream and egg noodles. Securely lock on cooker's lid, set cooker to HIGH, and cook 6 minutes.

SHOPPING LIST

1 tablespoon butter or margarine

1 pound lean ground beef

½ onion, diced

2 stalks celery, chopped

4 ounces mushrooms, sliced

1 teaspoon beef base (see page: 12) mixed into only ½ cup water

½ teaspoon garlic powder

½ teaspoon onion powder

¼ teaspoon allspice

1½ cups reduced fat sour cream

Salt and pepper to taste

Egg noodles, cooked separately

4. LET pressure release naturally 10 minutes before quick releasing remaining pressure and safely removing the lid. Stir in sour cream, salt and pepper to taste, and serve over egg noodles.

Bob's Tips

Egg noodles cook so fast that you can easily boil them on the stove as soon as the stroganoff is cooking in the pressure cooker, and everything should come out at the same time.

BEEF

SWEET AND SOUR MEATBALLS

NEXT TIME YOU FIND YOURSELF volunteered to bring a main dish for a potluck, make these easy and tasty meatballs. They're the perfect party food, and hold up well to reheating. With the effortless use of frozen meatballs, just don't tell anyone how you make them so perfectly round!

1. ADD all ingredients to pressure cooker; stir well. Securely lock on the lid, set cooker to HIGH, and cook 5 minutes.

2. LET pressure release naturally 10 minutes before (carefully!) quick releasing remaining pressure and safely removing the lid. Serve over rice.

SHOPPING LIST

2 pounds (32 ounces) frozen meatballs

½ onion, diced

¾ cup water

⅔ cup light brown sugar

1 cup ketchup

2 tablespoons vinegar

2 teaspoons lemon juice

2 tablespoons soy sauce

Bob's Tips

To make your own porcupine meatballs in place of the frozen meatballs: combine 1 pound ground beef with ½ cup uncooked long grain white rice, ½ cup water, ½ teaspoon onion powder, ¼ teaspoon garlic powder, and ¼ teaspoon ground black pepper. Increase cooking time by 1 minute.

PREP TIME	COOK TIME	SERVES	TEMPERATURE
10 MINS	65 MINS	FOUR-SIX	HIGH

BEEF

TRADITIONAL CORNED BEEF AND CABBAGE

Y OU NO LONGER HAVE TO WAIT HALF A DAY for this Irish favorite! Corned beef can be found in both "point" and "flat" cuts. I suggest a flat cut, as points tend to vary greatly in thickness, and contain more fat. Flat cuts also cut into nice even slices from one end to the other.

1. ADD corned beef, pickling spices, garlic, and bay leaf to pressure cooker, and cover with just enough water to sit parallel to the top of beef.

2. SECURELY lock on cooker's lid, set cooker to HIGH, and cook 60 minutes.

3. PERFORM a quick release to release cooker's pressure. Safely remove lid, and remove beef, letting it rest under aluminum foil 5 minutes.

4. WHILE beef is resting, add Vegetables to cooking liquid in cooker, cabbage last. Securely lock on lid, set cooker to HIGH, and cook 5 minutes.

5. PERFORM a quick release to release cooker's pressure. Slice corned beef against the meat's grain, and serve with vegetables. If meat dries out, spoon a small amount of cooking liquid over top to hydrate.

SHOPPING LIST

2-3 pounds corned beef with pickling spice packet

1 tablespoon minced garlic

1 bay leaf

VEGETABLES

6 small redskin potatoes, halved

2 cups baby carrots

1 small head cabbage, quartered

Bob's Tips

To keep the pickling spices from getting in between the leaves of the cabbage, you can tie the spices into cheesecloth before dropping them into the pot. A stainless steel tea steeping ball also works well. If your beef does not come with a packet of spices, you can add 1 tablespoon pickling spice, found in the spice aisle.

ORANGE PEPPER STEAK

THOUGH IT'S CALLED PEPPER STEAK, THIS recipe is more citrus than spice, and in only 12 minutes time, who needs those take out cartons? This no-stir, stir-fry is best served over white rice with a side of steamed broccoli.

1. ADD sesame and vegetable oils to pressure cooker, and heat on HIGH or "BROWN" with the lid off.

2. MIX salt and pepper into flour, and generously coat beef strips.

3. PLACE beef strips in pressure cooker, and lightly brown on all sides.

4. ADD remaining ingredients, except onion, bell peppers, and garnish. Securely lock on cooker's lid, set cooker to HIGH, and cook 8 minutes.

5. PERFORM a quick release to release cooker's pressure. Safely remove lid, and add onions and bell peppers.

6. SECURELY lock on cooker's lid, and cook on HIGH another 4 minutes.

7. PERFORM a quick release to release cooker's pressure. Safely remove lid, and serve topped with fresh orange slices.

SHOPPING LIST

1 tablespoon sesame oil

2 tablespoons vegetable oil

1 pound beef round steaks, cut into ½-inch strips

1 cup flour

½ teaspoon salt

½ teaspoon pepper

1 teaspoon beef base (see page: 12) mixed into 1 cup orange juice

2 teaspoons minced garlic

2 teaspoons fresh orange zest

3 tablespoons soy sauce

2 tablespoons sugar

½ white onion, peeled and sliced in ½-inch wide strips

1 green bell pepper, cored and sliced in ½-inch wide strips

1 red bell pepper, cored and sliced in ½-inch wide strips

Fresh orange slices, for garnish

Though you are zesting a fresh orange, it's best to buy store-bought orange juice for the juice in this recipe. It's much more concentrated than fresh, and adds a better flavor. Slice the fresh orange for the garnish!

BEEF

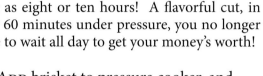

BEEF BRISKET ROAST

LONG, SLOW COOKING IS USUALLY THE key to this inexpensive cut of meat. Really long, and really slow cooking, sometimes as long as eight or ten hours! A flavorful cut, in only 60 minutes under pressure, you no longer have to wait all day to get your money's worth!

1. ADD brisket to pressure cooker, and cover with remaining ingredients, except cornstarch.

2. SECURELY lock on cooker's lid, set cooker to HIGH, and cook 60 minutes.

3. LET pressure release naturally 10 minutes before quick releasing remaining pressure and safely removing the lid.

4. REMOVE brisket, and set aside to rest under aluminum foil as you thicken the gravy.

SHOPPING LIST

1 (2- to 3-pound) brisket

1 teaspoon beef base (see page: 12) mixed into 1 cup water

2 cups water

1 tablespoon minced garlic

1 packet powdered onion soup mix

1 bay leaf

1 sprig fresh thyme or 1 teaspoon dried

2 tablespoons cornstarch

Salt and pepper to taste

5. To thicken gravy: set cooker to HIGH or "BROWN" with the lid off, until cooking juices are simmering. Mix cornstarch mixed with 2 tablespoons water, and slowly add to simmering juices, stirring constantly, until thick.

6. CARVE brisket thin, against the meat's grain, and serve smothered in gravy.

To ADD VEGETABLES: perform a quick release 55 minutes into the cooking time to cover brisket with large chunks of your favorite vegetables such as celery, carrots or halved new potatoes. Re-secure lid, and cook for 5 minutes on HIGH before letting the pressure release naturally, and following the rest of the recipe.

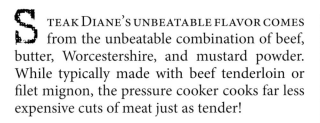

STEAK DIANE

STEAK DIANE'S UNBEATABLE FLAVOR COMES from the unbeatable combination of beef, butter, Worcestershire, and mustard powder. While typically made with beef tenderloin or filet mignon, the pressure cooker cooks far less expensive cuts of meat just as tender!

1. ADD butter and garlic to pressure cooker, and heat on HIGH or "BROWN" with the lid off, until sizzling.

2. PLACE steaks in pressure cooker, and lightly brown on both sides.

3. ADD beef base mixture, Worcestershire, dry mustard, and onion powder. Securely lock on cooker's lid, set cooker to HIGH, and cook 15 minutes.

4. PERFORM a quick release to release cooker's pressure before safely removing the lid. Add remaining ingredients, stir until well combined, and serve with your favorite potato dish.

SHOPPING LIST

2 tablespoons butter

1 teaspoon minced garlic

4 beef round steaks, about ¾ inch thick

½ teaspoon beef base (see page: 12) mixed into ½ cup water

1 tablespoon Worcestershire sauce

½ teaspoon dry mustard powder

¼ teaspoon onion powder

1 tablespoon brandy

⅓ cup heavy cream

1 tablespoon chopped chives

1 tablespoon parsley flakes

Salt and pepper to taste

This recipe is a bare bones version of the dish, ready for all kinds of quick and easy additions. Try adding ½ of a red onion, diced, or 2 to 3 shallots, diced, while browning the meat, and 8 ounces of halved mushrooms with the remaining ingredients for something even better!

SWEDISH MEATBALLS

With almost no prep time, and only a seven minute cook time, these Swedish Meatballs in sour cream gravy are "fast" food your family can really get behind. While you can make the meatballs yourself (see my tips below), the sour cream sauce is so rich with the flavors of traditional Swedish Meatballs that using frozen meatballs of any variety saves you time without compromising any taste. Plus, they easily stack on top of each other in the pressure cooker without losing their shape.

1. ADD all ingredients, except sour cream, to pressure cooker. Securely lock on the lid, set cooker to HIGH, and cook 7 minutes.

2. PERFORM a quick release to release cooker's pressure. Safely remove lid, and immediately stir in sour cream until well blended. Salt and pepper to taste, and serve immediately over egg noodles or alongside mashed or fingerling potatoes.

SHOPPING LIST

2 pounds (32 ounces) frozen meatballs

2 teaspoons beef base (see page: 12) mixed into 2 cups water

2 teaspoons minced garlic

1½ teaspoons onion powder

¼ teaspoon nutmeg

½ teaspoon allspice

1 tablespoon parsley flakes

16 ounces sour cream

Salt and pepper to taste

Bob's Tips

To make your own, fresh meatballs: combine 1 cup white bread crumbs with ½ cup heavy cream, and let sit 5 minutes. Mix into 1 pound lean ground beef, and then add 2 teaspoons onion powder, 2 tablespoons parsley, 2 teaspoons salt, ½ teaspoon pepper, and ⅛ teaspoon nutmeg.

CHIANTI POT ROAST WITH MUSHROOMS AND TOMATOES

THIS TWIST ON CLASSIC POT ROAST IS LIKE booking a one-way ticket to Tuscany for your taste buds.

1. ADD oil to pressure cooker, and heat on HIGH or "BROWN" with the lid off. Sprinkle both sides of roast with salt, garlic powder, and black pepper, then place roast in cooker to brown. Sear both sides, until browned.

2. POUR in ¾ cup Chianti, stab roast with a meat fork, and push meat around bottom of pan to release the glaze you've created.

3. ADD beef base mixture, tomato paste, sugar, minced garlic, and Italian seasoning. Securely lock on cooker's lid, set cooker to HIGH, and cook for 45 minutes.

4. PERFORM a quick release to release the cooker's pressure. Safely remove lid, then remove roast to rest under aluminum foil.

5. ADD mushrooms and tomatoes to cooker, and cook over HIGH heat with the lid off for 3–5 minutes; stir in remaining ¾ cup Chianti. To thicken sauce, combine cornstarch with 2 tablespoons water in a small dish, and stir into simmering sauce until thick. Serve over roast.

SHOPPING LIST

ROAST

4 tablespoons olive oil

1 (2- to 3-pound) beef chuck roast

½ teaspoon salt

½ teaspoon garlic powder

Ground black pepper to taste

1½ cups Chianti red wine, divided

1½ teaspoons beef base (see page: 12) mixed into 1½ cups water

3 ounces tomato paste (½ small can)

2 teaspoons sugar

2 tablespoons minced garlic

1½ teaspoons Italian seasoning

VEGETABLES

8 ounces baby bella mushrooms, sliced (sold pre-sliced in many stores)

4 medium tomatoes, cut in large chunks

2 tablespoons cornstarch

Bob's Tips This recipe goes great with fresh cheese tortellini found in the refrigerated case. Add them, plus an extra tablespoon beef base mixed with 1 cup water, to the sauce in the cooker when you add mushrooms and tomatoes, cooking 6–8 minutes, until they are tender.

BEEF

BEEF GOULASH

GOULASH IS ONE OF THE BEST, AND certainly one of the most recognizable dishes that Hungary has given us. While closely related to good old American beef stew, it's the paprika that really sets this dish apart.

1. ADD butter and bacon to pressure cooker, and heat on HIGH or "BROWN" with the lid off, until bacon begins to crisp.

2. PLACE garlic and beef cubes in cooker, and lightly brown on all sides.

3. ADD remaining ingredients, securely lock on cooker's lid, set cooker to HIGH, and cook for 15 minutes.

4. LET pressure release naturally 5 minutes before quick releasing remaining pressure and safely removing the lid.

5. To THICKEN: set cooker to HIGH or "BROWN" with lid off. Combine cornstarch with 2 tablespoons water in a small dish, and stir into simmering goulash until thick. Salt and pepper to taste, and serve over egg noodles or spaetzle.

SHOPPING LIST

1 tablespoon butter

2 slices raw bacon, diced

1 tablespoon minced garlic

1 pound beef round steaks, cut into ¾-inch cubes

1 red onion, diced

1 red bell pepper, chopped

1 green bell pepper, chopped

2 teaspoons beef base (see page: 12) mixed into 2 cups water

3 tablespoons tomato paste

Zest of ½ lemon

1 teaspoon dried marjoram

2 teaspoons paprika

1 teaspoon caraway seeds

2 tablespoons cornstarch

Salt and pepper to taste

Egg noodles or spaetzle, cooked separately

Bob's Tips

Hungarian or sweet paprika works best in this recipe, but regular paprika will do. Stewed vegetables such as carrots and potatoes work well in this dish. Cut them into large chunks, and interrupt the cooking process with a quick release to add them in 5 minutes before goulash is finished cooking.

WINE BRAISED SHORT RIBS WITH PRUNES

BEEF

W HEN IT COMES TO SHORT RIBS, I'M HERE to say that the buck does not stop at barbecue sauce. Very versatile, these ribs are not to be sold *short*. These wine braised ribs stew alongside prunes for a deep and somewhat fruity flavor that's out of this world!

1. ADD vegetable oil to pressure cooker, and heat on HIGH or "BROWN" with the lid off, until sizzling.

2. PLACE short ribs in cooker, and lightly brown on both sides.

3. COVER with remaining ingredients. Securely lock on cooker's lid, set cooker to HIGH, and cook 30 minutes.

4. LET pressure release naturally 10 minutes before quick releasing remaining pressure and safely removing the lid. Salt and pepper to taste, and serve.

SHOPPING LIST

2 tablespoons vegetable oil

3–4 pounds short ribs, trimmed of fat, and seasoned with pinches of salt and pepper

1 onion, halved then sliced ¼ inch thick

1 cup dry red wine

1 teaspoon beef base (see page: 12) mixed into 1 cup water

3 tablespoons tomato paste

1 tablespoon minced garlic

1 teaspoon Worcestershire sauce

12 pitted prunes

1 bay leaf

1 teaspoon dried thyme

Salt and pepper to taste

Bob's Tips

This recipe is also great with an extremely dark beer in place of the red wine. I like to use Guinness as it's just about as dark as beer gets!

BEEF

SLOPPY JOES

Sloppy Joes are about as comfort food as a sandwich gets. Like macaroni and cheese is to pasta—Sloppy Joes are to sandwiches—simple, satisfying, and something the whole family will enjoy. Serve alongside that macaroni and cheese, and take a trip down memory lane!

1. ADD vegetable oil to pressure cooker, and heat on HIGH or "BROWN" with the lid off, until sizzling. Add ground beef, breaking it up with spoon or spatula as it browns.

2. ONCE the ground beef is breaking up well, carefully drain most of the fat from pot, then add onion. Stir for 2 minutes, until onions start to turn translucent.

3. ADD remaining ingredients, except hamburger buns, and stir. Securely lock on cooker's lid, set cooker to HIGH, and cook 8 minutes.

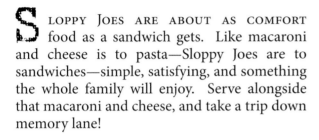

SHOPPING LIST

1 tablespoon vegetable oil

1 pound lean ground beef

1 onion, diced

½ cup ketchup

1 (6-ounce) can tomato paste

2 tablespoons light brown sugar

2 tablespoons yellow mustard

2 tablespoons vinegar

2 tablespoons Worcestershire sauce

½ cup water

Salt and pepper to taste

6 hamburger buns

4. LET pressure release naturally 10 minutes before quick releasing remaining pressure and safely removing the lid. Salt and pepper to taste, and serve on hamburger buns.

Bob's Tips

Try to purchase nice, large, and dense hamburger buns to hold up to a generous amount of the wonderful Sloppy Joe sauce. Lightly toast buns, and top with Cheddar cheese for that little extra touch.

BEEF

BEEF AND BARLEY STEW

A COLD WINTER NIGHT IS MUCH MORE bearable when you know you have a steaming hot bowl of beef stew to come home to. Even the smell will warm you up. Pair with some crusty French bread or even cornbread, and let it snow!

1. ADD all ingredients except peas, onion, mushrooms, and cornstarch to pressure cooker. Securely lock on the lid, set cooker to HIGH, and cook 20 minutes.

2. LET pressure release naturally 5 minutes before quick releasing remaining pressure and safely removing the lid.

3. SET cooker to HIGH or "BROWN" with the lid off. Add peas, onion, and mushrooms, and simmer 5 minutes.

4. POUR cornstarch mixture into simmering stew slowly until stew thickens to your liking. Salt and pepper to taste, and serve.

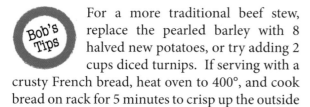 For a more traditional beef stew, replace the pearled barley with 8 halved new potatoes, or try adding 2 cups diced turnips. If serving with a crusty French bread, heat oven to 400°, and cook bread on rack for 5 minutes to crisp up the outside while warming the inside.

SHOPPING LIST

2 pounds chuck or round roast, cut into 1½-inch cubes

1 cup baby carrots

2 stalks celery, cut into 1½-inch pieces

⅓ cup pearled barley

1 tablespoon olive oil

4 teaspoons beef base (see page: 12) mixed into 4 cups water

½ cup red wine

2 tablespoons tomato paste

⅛ teaspoon ground allspice

1 tablespoon minced garlic

2 bay leaves

1 sprig fresh thyme, or 1 teaspoon dried

1 cup frozen peas

1 onion, peeled and sliced thin

8 ounces mushrooms, halved

2 tablespoons cornstarch, mixed into 2 tablespoons water

Salt and pepper to taste

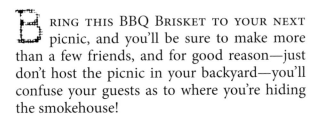

BBQ BRISKET

BRING THIS BBQ BRISKET TO YOUR NEXT picnic, and you'll be sure to make more than a few friends, and for good reason—just don't host the picnic in your backyard—you'll confuse your guests as to where you're hiding the smokehouse!

SHOPPING LIST

1 (2- to 3-pound) brisket

1 batch Stick to Your Ribs BBQ Sauce (recipe page: 187)

1 (12-ounce) can or bottle beer

2 teaspoons liquid smoke

1. ADD brisket to pressure cooker, and cover with remaining ingredients.

2. SECURELY lock on cooker's lid, set cooker to HIGH, and cook 50 minutes.

3. PERFORM a quick release to release cooker's pressure. Safely remove lid, and remove beef, letting it rest under aluminum foil 5 minutes.

4. SLICE brisket against the meat's grain, and serve smothered in sauce from cooker. Serve with your picnic favorites!

Bob's Tips

If you are in a pinch you can substitute a bottle of your favorite barbecue sauce in place of the Stick to Your Ribs BBQ Sauce…don't worry, I'll look the other way!

Beef Burgundy

BEEF

This traditional French dish, also known as Beef Bourguignon is a favorite of mine. Though the recipe has changed over the years, the key to all of its great flavors is still the same—browning the meat in butter and bacon fat before stewing it in wine.

1. Add butter, bacon, and garlic to pressure cooker, and heat on HIGH or "BROWN" with the lid off, until bacon begins to crisp.

2. Coat beef cubes with flour mixture. Place in pressure cooker, and lightly brown on all sides.

3. Add remaining ingredients, except ¾ cup Burgundy and cornstarch. Securely lock on cooker's lid, set cooker to HIGH, and cook 15 minutes.

4. Perform a quick release to release cooker's pressure before safely removing the lid. Stir in remaining ¾ cup Burgundy.

5. To thicken the sauce, set cooker to HIGH or "BROWN" with the lid off. Combine cornstarch with 2 tablespoons water in a small dish, and stir into simmering sauce until thick. Salt and pepper to taste, and serve over egg noodles or your favorite pasta or potato dish.

Shopping List

2 tablespoons butter

2 slices raw bacon, cut into ¼-inch pieces

1 tablespoon minced garlic

1 pound beef round steaks, cut into ¾-inch cubes

1 cup flour, mixed with pinches of salt and pepper

1½ cups Burgundy or dry red wine, divided

1 teaspoon beef base (see page: 12) mixed into 1 cup water

1 tablespoon tomato paste

8 ounces mushrooms, cleaned and halved

2 cups peeled white pearl onions

1 teaspoon dried tarragon

1 bay leaf

2 tablespoons cornstarch

Salt and pepper to taste

 Bob's Tips Typically, the herbs in this dish would be prepared into a bouquet garni—a little bundle of the fresh herbs you have on hand, bound together with string for easy retrieval at the end of the cooking process.

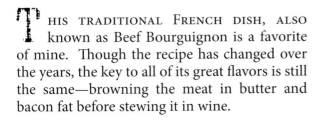
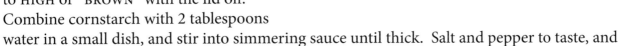

Cooking Times
Poultry

When cooking poultry, especially whole chickens or large turkey legs, and breasts, be sure to use a meat thermometer after cooking to check that the internal temperature has reached 180°. For better color and better tasting skin, brown the meat first.

Chicken	Size	Liquid	Cook Minutes	Temp
Breasts, bone in	any	½ cup	10	high
Breasts, boneless	any	½ cup	5	high
Cornish Hen	2 hens	1 cup	12	high
Legs	2 pounds	½ cup	7	high
Thighs	2 pounds	½ cup	7	high
Whole Chicken	3–4 pounds	2 cups	30	high
Wings	1–3 pounds	½ cup	7	high
Turkey				
Breast, bone in	3–5 pounds	2 cups	30	high
Breast, boneless	3–5 pounds	2 cups	25	high
Legs	2–4 legs	1½ cups	17	high

POULTRY

CHICKEN PICCATA

POULTRY

THIS CLASSIC ITALIAN DISH IS TANGY, TART, and delicious. In the pressure cooker, the buttery lemon and wine sauce infuses into the chicken for a ten-minute dinner that is bursting with all of the flavors of any fine restaurant.

1. DIP chicken breasts in lightly salted flour, until well coated.

2. ADD olive oil and butter to pressure cooker, and heat on HIGH or "BROWN" with the lid off, until sizzling. Place chicken breasts into cooker, browning them on both sides.

3. ADD onions and garlic, and cook until onions begin to sweat. Add remaining ingredients, except cornstarch, capers, and lemon garnish.

4. SECURELY lock on cooker's lid, set to HIGH, and cook 10 minutes.

5. PERFORM a quick release to release cooker's pressure. Safely remove lid, then remove chicken breasts, and set aside.

SHOPPING LIST

6 small boneless, skinless chicken breast halves (about 2 pounds)

½ cup flour, mixed with pinch of salt

2 tablespoons olive oil

2 tablespoons butter

½ red onion, diced

1 tablespoon minced garlic

1 teaspoon chicken base (see page: 12) mixed into 1 cup water

1 cup dry white wine

¼ cup lemon juice

¼ teaspoon white pepper

½ teaspoon Italian seasoning

1 tablespoon cornstarch

2 tablespoons capers, jarred

1 lemon, sliced thin, for garnish

6. THICKEN cooking liquid by combining cornstarch with 2 tablespoons water in a small dish, then stirring it into cooker on HIGH or "BROWN" with lid off, until thick. Return chicken into sauce to fully coat before serving. Serve topped with capers and fresh lemon slices.

Bob's Tips

Although store-bought lemon juice is easiest, fresh-squeezed lemon juice makes this recipe truly great. For a full meal, serve over well-oiled angel hair pasta with a side of steamed asparagus or broccoli.

CHICKEN THIGH OSSO BUCO

POULTRY

TYPICALLY MADE WITH VEAL OR LAMB shanks, this recipe for Osso Buco substitutes far cheaper chicken thighs without sacrificing any of the incredible Italian flavors you'd expect. The added bonus is that the dish is suddenly very kid friendly when you've got a whole family to please!

1. ADD olive oil to pressure cooker, and heat on HIGH or "BROWN" with the lid off.

2. COAT chicken thighs in seasoned flour before adding to cooker to lightly brown on both sides.

3. ADD garlic, onion, carrots, and celery, and sauté 1 minute before covering with remaining ingredients.

4. SECURELY lock on cooker's lid, set cooker to HIGH, and cook 10 minutes.

5. LET pressure release naturally 10 minutes before quick releasing remaining pressure and safely removing the lid. Salt and pepper to taste, and serve.

SHOPPING LIST

3 tablespoons olive oil

8 chicken thighs

1 cup flour mixed with pinches of salt and pepper

1 red onion, chopped

2 tablespoons minced garlic

2 carrots, cut into ¼-inch discs

2 stalks celery, chopped

1 teaspoon chicken base (see page: 12) mixed into ½ cup water

1 cup dry red wine

1 (14- to 16-ounce) can diced tomatoes

2 tablespoons tomato paste

2 teaspoons Italian seasoning

Salt and pepper to taste

Bob's Tips

Though the meat will be more tender with bone-in thighs, this can also be prepared with boneless, skinless chicken thighs for easier eating! Try serving with the traditional Osso Buco gremolata topping, recipe on page: 109.

PREP TIME	COOK TIME	SERVES	TEMPERATURE
15 MINS	14 MINS	FOUR	HIGH

CHICKEN WITH 40 CLOVES OF GARLIC

WHILE THIS RECIPE MAY AT FIRST SOUND like the kind of dish you'd want to avoid on a dinner date, the garlic cooks up mild, and soft; almost buttery. The consensus is that you absolutely must serve this with thin, toasted slices of a crusty bread to literally spread the creamy garlic cloves onto.

1. ADD olive oil and butter or margarine to pressure cooker, and heat on HIGH or "BROWN" with the lid off, until sizzling.

2. DIP chicken pieces in seasoned flour, coating well. Add to cooker, and lightly brown on all sides.

3. COVER with remaining ingredients. Securely lock on cooker's lid, set cooker to HIGH, and cook 14 minutes.

4. LET pressure release naturally 10 minutes before quick releasing remaining pressure and safely removing the lid.

SHOPPING LIST

2 tablespoons olive oil

2 tablespoons butter or margarine

2 pounds chicken pieces, bone in

½ cup flour, mixed with ½ teaspoon salt and ½ teaspoon pepper

4 stalks celery, cut into 2-inch lengths

40 cloves garlic, peeled

½ teaspoon chicken base (see page: 12) mixed into ½ cup water

¼ cup dry white wine

½ teaspoon dried rosemary

1 teaspoon dried thyme

Salt and pepper to taste

5. SALT and pepper chicken pieces to taste, serving them with tongs. Use a slotted spoon to serve celery and garlic cloves over top.

Most grocery stores sell garlic cloves that are already peeled, and ready to go in a small plastic jar usually found in the produce department's refrigerated salad case. One whole jar should be just enough for this recipe.

CHICKEN POT PIE

THIS CHUNKY COMFORT FOOD CLASSIC can't be made any easier or faster than this! The flaky puff pastry "crown" will make you feel like a king dipping into the creamy filling that is thickened with instant mashed potatoes!

1. PREHEAT oven to 400°. Place pastry sheet on sheet pan coated with nonstick spray. Place 4 individual serving bowls upside down on pastry sheet cut around circumference of the bowls. Discard trimmings (or save for another use).

2. PLACE remaining ingredients, except Parmesan cheese, heavy cream, potato flakes, and peas into cooker. Securely lock on the lid, set cooker to HIGH, and cook 5 minutes.

3. PLACE baking sheet with circular pastry tops into preheated oven, and bake 8–12 minutes, until golden brown.

4. WHEN the filling is finished cooking, let pressure release naturally 5 minutes before quick releasing remaining pressure and safely removing the lid. Stir in Parmesan cheese, heavy cream, potato flakes, and peas until thick and creamy. Salt and pepper to taste, and serve in individual bowls, each topped with a puff pastry top.

SHOPPING LIST

1 package frozen puff pastry sheets, thawed

Nonstick cooking spray

2 tablespoons butter or margarine

1 onion, chopped

3 boneless, skinless chicken breasts, cut into 3 strips then cubed

8 ounces mushrooms, sliced

2 carrots, cut into ¼-inch discs

1 teaspoon chicken base (see page: 12) mixed into 1 cup water

4 new red potatoes, cubed

½ teaspoon dried thyme

½ teaspoon poultry seasoning

1 bay leaf

1 teaspoon sugar

3 tablespoons grated Parmesan cheese

½ cup heavy cream

4 tablespoons instant potato flakes

1 cup frozen peas, thawed

Salt and pepper to taste

Bob's Tips

The trimmings left after cutting the circular puff pastry tops can be cut into small squares, and baked into light and fluffy croutons to top any soup or salad!

POULTRY

Shown with *Herb "Roasted" Summer Squash* (recipe page: 139)

CORNISH GAME HENS WITH GARLIC AND ROSEMARY

THIS CLASSIC ROASTING RECIPE IS ONLY missing one thing: the woe of waiting for a slow roasted dinner. I am here to report, however, that the flavors are all intact. The fragrant rosemary and intensely infused garlic is perfect for this pair of Cornish hens, and in only 12 minutes under pressure, the flavors would try to escape…if they had the time!

1. RINSE each hen well inside and out, then stuff cavity with 1 clove garlic and 1 lemon wedge. Truss back legs with baking twine, and tuck wings underneath body.

2. ADD Cooking Liquid ingredients to pressure cooker, and (for best results) place a metal rack in bottom of cooker to keep hens above liquid. Place hens on rack.

3. MIX Herb Rub ingredients in a small bowl, using the back of a spoon to press ingredients into the bowl, releasing the natural oils of the rosemary.

4. THOROUGHLY coat tops of hens with Herb Rub, securely lock on cooker's lid, set cooker to HIGH, and cook 12 minutes (15 if hens are very large).

SHOPPING LIST

2 Cornish game hens, giblets removed

2 cloves garlic

2 wedges lemon

COOKING LIQUID

½ teaspoon chicken base (see page: 12) mixed into ½ cup water

½ cup dry white wine

2 tablespoons lemon juice

1 tablespoon butter or margarine

1 teaspoon poultry seasoning

HERB RUB

2 tablespoons olive oil

2 tablespoons minced garlic

1 tablespoon parsley flakes

2 teaspoons fresh rosemary leaves

½ teaspoon salt

¼ teaspoon ground black pepper

5. LET pressure release naturally 10 minutes before quick releasing remaining pressure and safely removing the lid. Let hens rest 5 minutes before serving.

Bob's Tips

Try making an herb rub out of a combination of fresh herbs, such as thyme, rosemary, and sage. I make it a rule to crush any fresh herbs that are about to go bad into olive oil, and keep the rub refrigerated. It extends the life of your fresh herbs for weeks!

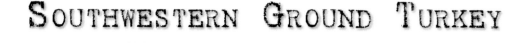

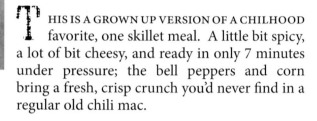

SOUTHWESTERN GROUND TURKEY MAC

POULTRY

THIS IS A GROWN UP VERSION OF A CHILHOOD favorite, one skillet meal. A little bit spicy, a lot of bit cheesy, and ready in only 7 minutes under pressure; the bell peppers and corn bring a fresh, crisp crunch you'd never find in a regular old chili mac.

1. ADD oil to pressure cooker, and heat on HIGH or "BROWN" with the lid off. Add ground turkey, breaking it up with a wooden spoon as it browns.

2. ONCE turkey is slightly browned, cover with remaining ingredients, except cheese, red bell pepper, and corn. Securely lock on cooker's lid, set cooker to HIGH, and cook 7 minutes.

3. PERFORM a quick release to release cooker's pressure. Safely remove lid, and stir in cheese, red bell pepper, and corn until cheese is completely melted. Salt and pepper to taste, and serve immediately.

SHOPPING LIST

1 tablespoon vegetable oil

1 pound ground turkey

2½ cups elbow macaroni

½ green bell pepper, diced

2 teaspoons chicken base (see page: 12) mixed into 2 cups water

½ cup water

½ teaspoon onion powder

¼ teaspoon chili powder

¼ teaspoon cayenne pepper

2 tablespoons butter or margarine

¾ pound processed cheese, cubed (such as Velveeta)

½ red bell pepper, diced small

1 cup frozen corn kernels

Salt and pepper to taste

Bob's Tips

Shopping for ground turkey is a little trickier than shopping for ground beef, as the fat content is not always as clearly labeled. I like to use ground turkey with 6–12g of fat per serving, often labeled as "lean." Ground turkey breast, with only 1 or 2g of fat is usable but much drier. Watch out for full fat ground turkey with as much as 20g of fat, even more than ground beef!

CHICKEN CACCIATORE

LITERALLY TRANSLATED FROM ITALIAN, this "hunter-style" dish is an easy way to prepare most any cut of chicken with boundless flavor. When I was growing up, this was one of those weeknight dishes I asked for regularly, even if I couldn't pronounce the name!

1. ADD olive oil to pressure cooker, and heat on HIGH or "BROWN" with the lid off, until sizzling.

2. COAT chicken breasts in seasoned flour before adding to cooker skin side down to lightly brown.

3. ADD remaining ingredients, except black olives. Securely lock on cooker's lid, set cooker to HIGH, and cook 10 minutes.

4. LET pressure release naturally 10 minutes before quick releasing remaining pressure and safely removing the lid. Add black olives to the pot, and salt and pepper to taste. Serve over rice or your favorite pasta.

SHOPPING LIST

3 tablespoons olive oil

4 chicken breasts, bone-in with skin

1 cup flour, mixed with pinches of salt, pepper, and paprika

1 onion, chopped large

1 green bell pepper, chopped large

2 tablespoons minced garlic

8 ounces mushrooms, cut in half

½ cup dry white wine

1 (14- to 16-ounce) can diced tomatoes

1 (8-ounce) can tomato sauce

3 tablespoons tomato paste

2 teaspoons Italian seasoning

1 cup pitted black olives

Salt and pepper to taste

Bob's Tips

Chicken fryer leg quarters can be substituted for the chicken breasts by upping the cooking time to 12 minutes. I like to buy leg quarters in bulk when they're on sale, and freeze them for just such recipes.

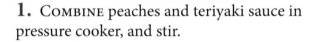

PEACHY KEEN CHICKEN

T HOUGH THE INGREDIENTS MAY SOUND like an odd combination, this sweet and savory dish is peachy keen with me! A quick and easy dinner, it's ready faster than you can pick a peach. Unless your kitchen is right under a peach tree that is—if so, you've got me there, but you should really use that peach to make the garnish!

SHOPPING LIST

6 small boneless, skinless chicken breast halves (about 2½ pounds)

2 (14- to 16-ounce) cans peach slices

2 tablespoons teriyaki sauce

1 tablespoon cornstarch

1. COMBINE peaches and teriyaki sauce in pressure cooker, and stir.

2. DIP chicken breasts in the mixture, then set them on top of peaches or insert a pressure cooker rack, if you have one, and set them on top of the rack.

3. SECURELY lock on cooker's lid, set cooker to HIGH, and cook 10 minutes.

4. PERFORM a quick release to release cooker's pressure. Safely remove lid, then remove chicken breasts, and set aside.

5. THICKEN the liquid and cooked peaches into a sauce by combining cornstarch with 2 tablespoons water in a small dish, and then stirring into cooker on HIGH or "BROWN" with the lid off, until thick.

6. RETURN chicken into sauce to fully coat before serving.

Bob's Tips

I like to boil instant white rice on the stove while the chicken is cooking. It's the perfect accompaniment for the Caribbean and Asian flair of this dish. If you own a grill pan, small indoor grill, or panini press; grilling sliced fresh peaches just long enough to mark them makes a most impressive garnish!

TURKEY TETRAZZINI

THIS CREAMY AND VERSATILE NO-BAKE "casserole" recipe is a great one to make when you've got leftover turkey in the fridge. If you don't have any leftover turkey, many stores sell pre-cooked turkey in cubes or strips. Or try making Chicken Tetrazzini with pre-cooked chicken strips or cubes found in any grocery store's refrigerated case. Tuna Tetrazzini can be made by foregoing the turkey, and stirring in 2 well-drained cans of tuna during the last step of the recipe.

1. ADD noodles, chicken base mixture, turkey, butter, and mushrooms to pressure cooker. Securely lock on the lid, set cooker to HIGH, and cook 4 minutes.

2. PERFORM a quick release to release cooker's pressure. Safely remove lid, and slowly stir in Swiss cheese, Parmesan cheese, sour cream, and peas until cheeses are melted and creamy. Salt and pepper to taste, and serve immediately, topped with cracker crumbs.

SHOPPING LIST

4 cups egg noodles, uncooked

3 teaspoons chicken base (see page: 12) mixed into 3 cups water

2 cups chopped or cubed cooked turkey

2 tablespoons butter or margarine

8 ounces mushrooms, sliced

1 cup shredded Swiss cheese

¼ cup grated Parmesan cheese

1 cup sour cream

¾ cup frozen peas, thawed

1 cup crumbled crackers (Ritz suggested)

Salt and pepper to taste

POULTRY

Bob's Tips More traditional Turkey Tetrazzini almost always contains some form of wine. Try adding ¼ cup dry sherry during the first step of cooking for something different and delicious; just keep in mind that wine isn't always a hit with younger kids!

CREAMY CHICKEN CURRY

POULTRY

WHILE "CURRY" IS A GENERIC TERM FOR a very broad variety of harmoniously spiced dishes, this recipe with a yogurt sauce is one of the more popular to be served in the Indian restaurants of North America. In the unlikely event that you have leftovers, this dish also makes a great base for chicken salad.

1. ADD vegetable oil to pressure cooker, and heat on HIGH or "BROWN" with the lid off, until sizzling.

2. DIP chicken breasts in seasoned flour, until well coated. Add to cooker, and lightly brown on both sides.

3. COVER with remaining ingredients, except yogurt and cornstarch. Securely lock on cooker's lid, set cooker to HIGH, and cook 8 minutes.

SHOPPING LIST

2 tablespoons vegetable oil

4 boneless, skinless chicken breasts

½ cup flour, mixed with ½ teaspoon salt and ½ teaspoon pepper

1 small onion, diced

1 teaspoon chicken base (see page: 12) mixed into 1 cup water

3 teaspoons curry powder

1 cup plain yogurt

1 tablespoon cornstarch

Additional curry powder to taste

4. LET pressure release naturally 10 minutes before quick releasing remaining pressure and safely removing the lid.

5. USE tongs to set aside chicken breasts while you make the creamy curry sauce. To make the sauce: set cooker to HIGH or "BROWN" with the lid off, and wait until cooking liquid is simmering. Thoroughly combine yogurt and cornstarch, then slowly stir into simmering liquid until fully integrated and sauce is creamy and thick. Add any additional curry powder to taste, dip chicken breasts in sauce, and serve with additional sauce poured over top.

Bob's Tips

With such a robust flavor, you may want to start with only 2 teaspoons of curry, and experiment with different levels, adding in a little at a time until you find the amount that is right for your palate.

CHICKEN BREAST COQ AU VIN

THE WONDERFULLY RICH FLAVORS OF France all come together in this hearty dish. In fact, it is so French that you may find yourself kissing your fingers, and donning a beret. Thankfully, it is not French enough to dress as a mime!

1. ADD butter, bacon, and garlic to pressure cooker, and heat on HIGH or "BROWN" with lid off, until bacon begins to crisp.

2. DREDGE chicken breasts in seasoned flour until well coated. Add to cooker, and lightly brown on both sides.

3. ADD remaining ingredients, except cornstarch. Securely lock on cooker's lid, set cooker to HIGH, and cook 10 minutes.

4. PERFORM a quick release to release cooker's pressure before safely removing the lid. To thicken sauce: set cooker to HIGH or "BROWN" with the lid off. Combine cornstarch with 2 tablespoons water in a small dish, and stir into simmering sauce until thick. Salt and pepper to taste, and serve with potatoes or over egg noodles, garnished with fresh parsley.

SHOPPING LIST

1 tablespoon butter or margarine

2 slices raw bacon, cut into ¼-inch pieces

1 tablespoon minced garlic

2–3 pounds boneless, skinless chicken breasts

1 cup flour, seasoned with pinches of salt and pepper

2 stalks celery, chopped

2 cups Burgundy wine

1 teaspoon beef base (see page: 12) mixed into 1 cup water

2 tablespoons tomato paste

8 ounces mushrooms, cleaned, and halved

2 cups white pearl onions, peeled

1 sprig fresh thyme or 1 teaspoon dried

1 bay leaf

2 tablespoons cornstarch

Salt and pepper to taste

Fresh parsley, for garnish

Bob's Tips

Typically, the herbs in this dish would be prepared into a bouquet garni—a little bundle of the fresh herbs you have on hand, bound together with string for easy retrieval at the end of the cooking process. I use a stainless steel tea steeping ball.

POULTRY

Shown with *Maple Butter Glazed Carrots*, page 146.

HONEY DIJON CHICKEN THIGHS

POULTRY

THIS CHICKEN RECIPE IS ONE OF THOSE super fast, super easy, and super crowd pleasing family dinners that kids will ask for time and time again. Mix up double the Dijon mustard, honey, brown sugar, salt, and pepper, and save half for a wonderful dipping sauce!

1. COMBINE all ingredients, except chicken base mixture, in pressure cooker's removable pot (for electronic cookers) or regular pressure cooker pot, and stir to evenly coat chicken. Cover, and refrigerate at least 30 minutes to marinate.

2. ONCE marinated, add chicken base mixture, securely lock on cooker's lid, set cooker to HIGH, and cook 8 minutes.

SHOPPING LIST

8 boneless, skinless chicken thighs

5 tablespoons Dijon mustard

2 tablespoons honey

1 tablespoon light brown sugar

½ teaspoon salt

¼ teaspoon ground black pepper

½ teaspoon chicken base (see page: 12) mixed into ½ cup water

3. LET pressure release naturally 10 minutes before quick releasing remaining pressure and safely removing the lid. Use tongs to remove thighs, and serve alongside rice or your favorite sides.

Bob's Tips

While boneless chicken thighs are more family friendly and easy to eat, bone-in thighs are typically much cheaper, especially when on sale, and can be substituted without any change in cooking time. Four boneless, skinless chicken breasts can also be substituted in a pinch.

CHICKEN MARSALA

POULTRY

Your guests will be looking for the Chianti bottle and the red and white checked tablecloth when you serve them this classic Italian entrée. The Marsala wine, which gives the dish its name, combines with mushrooms and chicken to provide a no-fuss, satisfying meal. Accordion music extra.

1. Add olive oil and butter to pressure cooker, and heat on HIGH or "BROWN" with the lid off, until sizzling.

2. Dip chicken breasts in seasoned flour, until well coated. Add to cooker, and brown well on both sides.

3. Pour in ½ cup Marsala wine, chicken base mixture, and mushrooms. Securely lock on cooker's lid, set cooker to HIGH, and cook 10 minutes.

4. Perform a quick release to release cooker's pressure and safely remove the lid.

SHOPPING LIST

1 tablespoon olive oil

2 tablespoons butter

6 small boneless, skinless chicken breast halves (about 2 pounds)

½ cup flour, mixed with ½ teaspoon salt and ½ teaspoon pepper

1 cup Marsala wine (or similar dry red wine), divided

1 teaspoon chicken base (see page: 12) mixed into 1 cup water

16 ounces mushrooms, cut in half

2 tablespoons cornstarch, mixed into ¼ cup milk

Salt and pepper to taste

5. Set cooker to HIGH or "BROWN" with the lid off, and add remaining ½ cup Marsala wine and cornstarch mixture. Stir constantly until sauce has thickened, then salt and pepper to taste. Serve over your favorite pasta.

Using whole milk or heavy cream to mix with the cornstarch at the end of cooking makes this dish even more decadent. Though white button mushrooms are cheapest and easiest to find, I would highly suggest baby bella mushrooms for their richer flavor.

POULTRY

TURKEY TENDERLOIN WITH CRANBERRY ORANGE GLAZE

WITH THIS TURKEY RECIPE, THERE'S NO worrying about whether or not the turkey will fit into a pressure cooker! Turkey tenderloin is arguably the moistest part of the turkey and slices into perfect "medallions" every time.

SHOPPING LIST

1 cup water

½ cup orange marmalade

1 cup frozen cranberries

¼ cup sugar

1 turkey tenderloin

2 tablespoons cornstarch

1. COMBINE water, orange marmalade, cranberries, and sugar in pressure cooker, and stir.

2. PLACE turkey tenderloin over top of mixture in cooker. Securely lock on cooker's lid, set cooker to HIGH, and cook 15 minutes.

3. PERFORM a quick release to release cooker's pressure. Safely remove lid, then remove tenderloin, setting aside to rest under aluminum foil.

4. THICKEN the glaze by combining cornstarch with 2 tablespoons water in a small dish, and stirring it into cooker on HIGH or "BROWN" with the lid off, simmering until thick.

5. CARVE turkey loin, and serve drizzled with glaze.

Bob's Tips

Many stores only carry turkey tenderloins pre-marinated in a range of different flavors. This isn't necessarily a bad thing as lemon pepper marinated turkey tenderloin goes quite well in the glaze.

PAPRIKA CHICKEN IN SOUR CREAM GRAVY

THIS HUNGARIAN DISH IS AN EXCITING way to spruce up dinner with ease. It's seemingly exotic while utilizing everyday ingredients that you may already have in the cupboard! So get cooking!

1. ADD butter to pressure cooker, and heat on HIGH or "BROWN" with the lid off, until sizzling.

2. DIP chicken breasts in seasoned flour, coating well. Add chicken to cooker, lightly browning on both sides before adding onion and garlic; sauté 2–3 minutes more.

3. COVER with remaining ingredients, except sour cream and cornstarch. Securely lock on cooker's lid, set cooker to HIGH, and cook 8 minutes.

4. LET pressure release naturally 10 minutes before quick releasing remaining pressure and safely removing the lid.

SHOPPING LIST

2 tablespoons butter or margarine

½ cup flour, mixed with ½ teaspoon salt and ½ teaspoon pepper, and 1 tablespoon paprika

4 boneless, skinless chicken breasts

1 small onion, diced

2 teaspoons minced garlic

1 teaspoon chicken base (see page: 12) mixed into 1 cup water

1 cup reduced-fat sour cream

1 tablespoon cornstarch

Salt and pepper to taste

Chopped fresh parsley, for garnish

Additional paprika, for garnish

5. USE tongs to set aside chicken breasts. Make sauce by setting cooker to HIGH or "BROWN" with the lid off, and wait until cooking liquid is simmering. Thoroughly combine sour cream and cornstarch, then slowly stir into simmering liquid until fully integrated and sauce is creamy and thick. Salt and pepper to taste, dip chicken breasts in sauce, and serve topped with chopped parsley and a pinch of paprika.

Hungarian or sweet paprika works best in this recipe if your local store stocks it, but regular paprika has worked just fine for me.

Shown with *Sesame Fried Rice*, page 166.

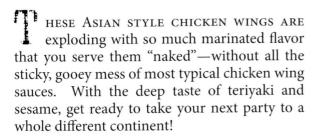

TERIYAKI CHICKEN WINGS

THESE ASIAN STYLE CHICKEN WINGS ARE exploding with so much marinated flavor that you serve them "naked"—without all the sticky, gooey mess of most typical chicken wing sauces. With the deep taste of teriyaki and sesame, get ready to take your next party to a whole different continent!

1. COMBINE all ingredients, except 2 tablespoons sesame oil and toasted sesame seeds, in a large bowl, and cover with plastic wrap. Refrigerate at least 2 hours (overnight recommended) to marinate.

2. HEAT remaining 2 tablespoons sesame oil in pressure cooker on HIGH or "BROWN" with the lid off, until sizzling.

SHOPPING LIST

2 pounds chicken wings, drum and wings separated

6 tablespoons sesame oil, divided

1 cup low-sodium teriyaki sauce

1 tablespoon lemon juice

2 tablespoons sugar

½ teaspoon crushed red pepper, optional

Toasted sesame seeds, for garnish

3. USING tongs, remove chicken wings from marinade (reserving marinade), and place in cooker to brown. Stir, lightly browning as many of the wings on as many sides as possible.

4. POUR marinade over browned wings, securely lock on cooker's lid, set cooker to HIGH, and cook 7 minutes.

5. LET pressure release naturally 10 minutes before quick releasing any remaining pressure, and safely remove lid. Remove with tongs, and serve topped with toasted sesame seeds.

Bob's Tips

To toast raw sesame seeds: heat them in a pan on the stove over medium heat until golden brown, about 4 minutes. Be sure to shake the pan constantly to keep them moving.

POULTRY

COOKING TIMES
PORK AND HAM

WHEN COOKING PORK roasts, browning the meat first is recommended. Let the pressure release naturally for 10 minutes for more tender meat. If hams are too large to fit into your cooker, they can be carefully cut off the bone in large sections before cooking (lower the cooking time to 30 minutes).

PORK	SIZE	LIQUID	COOK MINUTES	TEMP
BABY BACK RIBS	2–4 pounds	1 cup	20	HIGH
CHOPS	½-inch thick	½ cup	7	HIGH
CHOPS	1-inch thick	½ cup	15	HIGH
LOIN	3–5 pounds	2 cups	50	HIGH
ROASTS	3–5 pounds	2 cups	45	HIGH
SAUSAGES, RAW	1–3 pounds	to cover	10	HIGH
SPARERIBS	2–4 pounds	1 cup	10	HIGH
HAM				
HOCKS	any	to cover	60	HIGH
STEAKS	4 steaks	1 cup	8	HIGH
WHOLE, COOKED	4–6 pounds	3 cups	40	HIGH

PORK AND HAM

TWO CAN COLA PORK ROAST

THIS SPECTACULAR PORK ROAST RECIPE IS by far the greatest mystery in this book. Just how can cola make gravy that is this good? I'm not sure that even I know the answer, but I do know that it's delicious, and definitely not as sweet as you would think it to be.

SHOPPING LIST

1 (2- to 3-pound) pork loin, shoulder or butt

2 (12-ounce) cans regular cola (you know, the one in the red can)

1 packet powdered onion soup mix

2 tablespoons cornstarch

1. PLACE roast and all ingredients, except cornstarch, into pressure cooker. Securely lock on the lid, set cooker to HIGH, and cook 40 minutes.

2. LET pressure release naturally 10 minutes before quick releasing any remaining pressure and safely removing the lid.

3. CHECK roast for tenderness. If not fork-tender, re-secure the lid, and cook on HIGH an additional 10 minutes, with a 10-minute natural release.

4. REMOVE roast to rest under aluminum foil as you thicken the gravy. To thicken gravy: set cooker to HIGH or "BROWN" with lid off, until cooking juices are simmering. Mix cornstarch with 2 tablespoons water, and slowly add to simmering juices, stirring constantly until thick.

5. CARVE roast, and serve with plenty of gravy.

I like a good pork roast with mashed potatoes and fresh green beans, but if you'd like to make this into a one-pot meal, throw in your favorite vegetables when you remove the roast to rest. Five minutes under HIGH pressure is a pretty safe amount of time for quartered potatoes and large chunked carrots or celery.

PORK VINDALOO

D UST OFF YOUR ADVENTUROUS STREAK for this traditional Indian curry dish that is plentifully spiced and ready to take your taste buds for a ride! While Vindaloo has a reputation for being HOT, don't let that scare you off, as this recipe is a relatively mild variation.

1. COMBINE all ingredients, except chicken base mixture, in pressure cooker's removable pot (for electronic cookers) or regular pressure cooker pot, and stir to evenly coat. Cover, and refrigerate at least 2 hours to marinate.

2. ONCE marinated, add chicken base mixture. Securely lock on cooker's lid, set cooker to HIGH, and cook 15 minutes.

3. LET pressure release naturally 10 minutes before quick releasing remaining pressure and safely removing the lid. Salt and pepper to taste, and serve over rice.

SHOPPING LIST

2 pounds boneless pork loin, cut into 1-inch cubes

1 onion, diced

2 tablespoons olive oil

1 tablespoon minced garlic

¼ cup red wine vinegar

1 teaspoon ground dry mustard

½ teaspoon cumin

½ teaspoon ground cloves

¼ teaspoon chili powder

½ teaspoon ground cinnamon

½ teaspoon ground cardamom

1 teaspoon ground turmeric

½ teaspoon ground ginger

1 teaspoon sugar

1 teaspoon chicken base (see page: 12) mixed into 1 cup water

Salt and pepper to taste

Bob's Tips

If your spice rack isn't full to the hilt, you can substitute 3 teaspoons of curry powder in place of all of the spice ingredients except for the cinnamon in this recipe.

PORK LOIN CHOPS WITH APPLE AND SHERRY

PORK

I T'S NO SECRET THAT PORK AND APPLE ARE meant to be together. In this recipe, the juicy, boneless pork loin chops cook surrounded by thick-cut apples, sherry, cinnamon, and a touch of brown sugar for a sweet note that's delicious but not overwhelming. Serve this in the fall when apples are at their peak.

1. ADD oil to pressure cooker, and heat on HIGH or "BROWN" with the lid off, until sizzling.

2. ADD pork chops and onion, and sauté until chops are lightly browned on both sides.

3. COVER with remaining ingredients. Securely lock on cooker's lid, set cooker to HIGH, and cook 14 minutes.

4. PERFORM a quick release to release cooker's pressure. Safely remove lid, salt and pepper to taste, and serve drizzled with cooking liquid.

SHOPPING LIST

2 tablespoons vegetable oil

4 pork loin chops, 1-inch thick center-cut

½ red onion, diced

2 large apples, peeled, cored, and cut into 8 wedges each

½ cup dry sherry

½ teaspoon chicken base (see page: 12) mixed into ½ cup water

2 tablespoons butter

1 tablespoon brown sugar

¼ teaspoon cinnamon

Salt and pepper to taste

Bob's Tips

Any cut of pork chop will work well in this recipe, boneless or bone-in. You can even save money by buying the entire pork loin, and cutting the chops off yourself, freezing the rest of the loin for future meals!

Shown with *Honey Baked Beans*, page 127.

PULLED PORK SANDWICHES

PREPARING PULLED PORK TRADITIONALLY requires smoking 8 hours. The pressure cooker brings the cooking time down to 90 minutes, you can actually have your picnic lunch in time…for lunch.

1. COMBINE all Dry Rub ingredients in a small bowl.

2. CUT pork into 2-inch thick pieces (to speed up cooking time), then cut ⅛ inch deep, crisscrossing grooves into the pieces. Coat pieces with Dry Rub, pushing it into the grooves. Let sit 5 minutes.

3. ADD chicken base mixture and liquid smoke to pressure cooker. Place pork pieces over top, as separated as possible.

4. POUR BBQ Sauce over top. Securely lock on cooker's lid, set cooker to HIGH, and cook 90 minutes.

5. LET pressure release naturally at least 10 minutes before quick releasing any remaining pressure and safely removing the lid. Pork should be fork-tender and shred easily. If not, re-secure the lid, and cook an additional 20 minutes on HIGH.

SHOPPING LIST

DRY RUB

1 tablespoon chili powder

2 teaspoons ground cumin

½ teaspoon ground allspice

2 teaspoons salt

1 teaspoon ground black pepper

PULLED PORK

1 (4- to 5-pound) pork shoulder or butt

1 teaspoon chicken base (see page: 12) mixed into 1 cup water

1 teaspoon liquid smoke

1 batch Stick to Your Ribs BBQ Sauce (recipe page: 187)

SANDWICHES

Sesame seed buns

Sliced red onion, optional

Cheddar cheese slices, optional

PORK

6. SERVE pulled apart on sesame seed buns with your favorite toppings.

Bob's Tips

You can use a bottle of your favorite sauce, and 4 tablespoons tomato paste in place of my Stick to Your Ribs BBQ Sauce.

BABY BACK RIBS

NOTHING SAYS COMFORT QUITE LIKE THIS flavorful dish. The combination of tangy barbecue sauce and tender meat will satisfy the heartiest of appetites. Serve with coleslaw and corn on the cob, and you'll have a picnic lunch. Pair with mashed potatoes and green beans, and you have a full-fledged country supper.

SHOPPING LIST

½ cup water

3 pounds baby back pork ribs

1 batch Stick to Your Ribs BBQ Sauce (recipe
   page: 187)

1. ADD water to pressure cooker.

2. CUT ribs into sections small enough to fit into cooker, and generously coat with BBQ sauce. Lean ribs against the sides, standing upright in cooker.

3. ADD any remaining BBQ sauce to water at bottom of cooker. Securely lock on cooker's lid, set cooker to HIGH, and cook 20 minutes.

4. PERFORM a quick release to release cooker's pressure. Safely remove lid, and serve.

To give the ribs a little more color (and flavor), place cooked ribs on a sheet pan under the broiler for a few minutes until the sugars in the sauce begin to char. My Stick to Your Ribs BBQ Sauce is extra thick to withstand the extra liquid of pressure cooking, but you can use a bottle of your favorite sauce and 4 tablespoons tomato paste in its place for the same spectacular results.

PORK

MOJO MARINATED PORK ROAST

THIS ISLAND SPICED PORK ROAST GETS all of its amazing citrus, garlic, and fresh herb flavors from a marinade called mojo criollo, which you can find in the marinades section (usually near the condiments) of your local grocery store. If you are having trouble finding it, check the ethnic aisle of your store, and you should be in luck!

SHOPPING LIST

1 (2- to 4-pound) pork roast

1 bottle mojo criollo marinade (minimum 12 ounces)

2 tablespoons vegetable oil

½ teaspoon chicken base (see page: 12) mixed into ½ cup water

PORK

1. MARINATE roast in mojo criollo marinade, covered and refrigerated at least 2 hours before preparing to cook.

2. ADD oil to pressure cooker, and heat on HIGH or "BROWN" with the lid off, until sizzling.

3. REMOVE roast from marinade, reserving marinade. Place roast in cooker, and brown on both top and bottom.

4. POUR in chicken base mixture and reserved marinade. Securely lock on cooker's lid, set cooker to HIGH, and cook 40 minutes.

5. LET pressure release naturally 10 minutes before quick releasing any remaining pressure and safely removing the lid. Roast should be fork-tender. If not, re-lock on the lid, and cook on HIGH an additional 10 minutes. Remove roast, and let rest under aluminum foil 5 minutes before carving. Traditionally, the roast is shredded into large chunks by fork, not sliced. Serve drizzled with cooking liquid to keep moist.

Though the roast will taste best when browned, you can make this recipe even easier by marinating the roast straight in the pressure cooker pot and skipping all the way to step 4 to cook. You'll create less dishes and get dinner to the table even faster!

94

HAM STEAKS WITH PINEAPPLE CHERRY GLAZE

YOU DON'T NEED TO SPEND ALL DAY BAKING a ham to have a delicious glazed ham dinner. This recipe is as simple and quick as it gets, with a sweet and tangy glaze made all the better by releasing the ham's natural juices as it cooks under pressure.

1. ADD juice from pineapple rings and maraschino cherries to pressure cooker, setting aside the rings and cherries for later. Add brown sugar and water, and stir.

2. FOR best results, place a metal rack over liquid, and set ham steaks on top of rack. Securely lock on cooker's lid, set cooker to HIGH, and cook 5 minutes.

3. LET pressure release naturally 5 minutes before quick releasing remaining pressure and safely removing the lid. Set aside ham steaks to rest under aluminum foil, and carefully remove metal rack with tongs.

4. SWITCH cooker to HIGH or "BROWN" with the lid off, until liquid is simmering. Mix orange juice and cornstarch in a small bowl until well combined, then slowly stir into simmering liquid in cooker to thicken and create the glaze.

5. ADD pineapple rings and cherries to the glaze to warm up, then serve over ham steaks with your favorite sides.

SHOPPING LIST

1 (20-ounce) can pineapple rings, juice and rings separated

1 (6- to 10-ounce) jar maraschino cherries, juice and cherries separated

2 tablespoons light brown sugar

¼ cup water

2 large ham steaks, about ¾ inch thick, cut in half

½ cup orange juice

1 tablespoon cornstarch

Bob's Tips For the best presentation, serve each ham steak with one or two pineapple rings, maraschino cherries sitting in the center of the rings. When shopping, ham steaks with the bone-in retain all of the texture of a full baked ham, while boneless ham steaks tend to have more in common with luncheon meat than a true baked ham.

PORK LOIN WITH MILK GRAVY

WHILE THE IDEA OF SIMMERING A PORK loin in milk may sound strange, it really highlights the wonderful flavors of the meat itself. In fact, the flavors it brings out are so wonderful that a tiny pinch of rosemary is the only herb in the dish!

1. ADD butter, oil, and pork loin to pressure cooker, and heat on HIGH or "BROWN" with the lid off, until loin is lightly browned on all sides.

2. COVER with remaining ingredients, except milk and cornstarch. Securely lock on cooker's lid, set cooker to HIGH, and cook 40 minutes.

3. LET pressure release naturally 10 minutes before quick releasing remaining pressure and safely removing the lid.

SHOPPING LIST

2 tablespoons butter

1 tablespoon vegetable oil

1 (2- to 3-pound) pork loin

1 tablespoon minced garlic

1 cup dry white wine

1 teaspoon chicken base (see page: 12) mixed into 1 cup water

¼ teaspoon dried rosemary

1 cup whole milk

2 tablespoons cornstarch

Salt and pepper to taste

4. ADD milk, and set cooker to HIGH or "BROWN" with the lid off. Simmer 10 minutes.

5. REMOVE roast to rest under aluminum foil as you thicken the gravy. To thicken gravy: mix cornstarch with 2 tablespoons water, and slowly add to simmering juices, stirring constantly, until thick. Salt and pepper to taste.

6. CARVE roast, and serve with plenty of gravy.

The longer you simmer the pork in the milk after cooking under pressure, the better the gravy will turn out.

BEER BRATS AND SAUERKRAUT

YOU DON'T HAVE TO BE FROM WISCONSIN to enjoy this traditional German take on the hot dog. A common staple of tailgate parties, this dish can help get a football fan through that long stretch between the NFL draft and the start of football season. Just make sure you have plenty of hot mustard on hand, and save some of the beer to drink with the brats.

1. ADD bratwurst, onion, butter, beer, and ⅓ of the sauerkraut to pressure cooker.

2. SECURELY lock on cooker's lid, set cooker to HIGH, and cook 10 minutes.

SHOPPING LIST

2 pounds bratwurst sausages

½ white onion, halved, then sliced thin

2 tablespoons butter or margarine

2 (12-ounce) bottles or cans beer

1 (24-ounce) can or bag sauerkraut

1 (6-count) package Hoagie rolls

PORK

3. PERFORM a quick release to release cooker's pressure. Safely remove lid, and stir in remaining sauerkraut. Serve with a slotted spoon into Hoagie rolls.

Bob's Tips

The water in the onions and sauerkraut has a tendency to dilute the beer, so while a lager is more typical of beer brats, I say that the darker the beer the better! Guinness Irish Stout is as dark as coffee, and will most certainly give you the most bang for your buck!

Shown with *Tzatziki Sauce* (recipe page: 182)

PORK SOUVLAKI

THOUGH SOUVLAKI KEBABS ARE USUALLY grilled, this recipe has all of the traditional flavors of oregano, olive oil, garlic, and lemon in less time than you can preheat a grill! Warm some pita bread in a 300° oven while the Souvlaki is cooking, and put it all together with my Tzatziki Sauce, and it may be something new (unless you've been to any diner in New England!), but I guarantee that you'll be back for seconds!

1. COMBINE all ingredients, except chicken base mixture, skewers, pita bread, and Tzatziki sauce in pressure cooker's removable pot (for electronic cookers), or regular pressure cooker pot, and stir to evenly coat. Cover, and refrigerate at least 2 hours to marinate.

2. ONCE marinated, add chicken base mixture. Securely lock on cooker's lid, set cooker to HIGH, and cook 10 minutes.

SHOPPING LIST

1½ pounds boneless pork loin, cut into 1-inch cubes

3 tablespoons olive oil

¼ cup lemon juice

1 tablespoon minced garlic

2 tablespoons dried oregano

¼ teaspoon salt

¼ teaspoon ground black pepper

½ teaspoon chicken base (see page: 12) mixed into ½ cup water

Bamboo skewers, optional

Pita bread, optional

Tzatziki Sauce (recipe page: 182)

3. LET pressure release naturally 10 minutes before quick releasing remaining pressure and safely removing the lid. Use tongs or a slotted spoon to remove pork from liquid. Let cool 2–3 minutes before threading pork onto bamboo skewers and serving with warm pita bread and Tzatziki Sauce.

Bob's Tips

Another typical way of eating Souvlaki is right on the pita, topped with a generous amount of Tzatziki sauce, fresh-sliced tomatoes, and red onion. It is also commonly served over rice pilaf. In New England diners, you're sure to get a small Greek salad on the side.

PORK

PORK POT ROAST

PORK

T HIS CLASSIC FAMILY MEAL IS LIKE TWO recipes in one. The first is the pot roast dinner, and the second is the sliced pork or Cuban sandwich made from the leftovers!

1. ADD oil to pressure cooker, and heat on HIGH or "BROWN" with the lid off, until sizzling. Brown seasoned roast on all sides.

2. ADD remaining Roast ingredients to cooker. Securely lock on cooker's lid, set cooker to HIGH, and cook 40 minutes.

3. LET pressure release naturally 10 minutes before quick releasing remaining pressure and safely removing the lid.

4. ADD Vegetables ingredients, except cornstarch, and re-lock on the lid. Set cooker to HIGH, and cook 5 more minutes.

5. PERFORM a quick release to release cooker's pressure. Safely remove lid, and set aside roast to rest under aluminum foil. To thicken gravy: set cooker to HIGH or "BROWN" with lid off, until juices are simmering. Mix cornstarch with 2 tablespoons water, and add slowly, stirring constantly until thick. Carve roast, and serve with vegetables and gravy.

SHOPPING LIST

ROAST

4 tablespoons vegetable oil

1 (2- to 3-pound) pork loin, shoulder or butt, seasoned with ½ teaspoon salt and pepper

½ cup dry white wine

2 teaspoons chicken base (see page: 12) mixed into 2 cups water

2 tablespoons minced garlic

1 sprig fresh thyme, or 1 teaspoon dried

2 bay leaves

VEGETABLES

6 small redskin potatoes, halved

2 small onions, peeled and quartered

1 cup baby carrots

2 stalks celery, cut into 1-inch pieces

Salt and pepper to taste

2 tablespoons cornstarch

This recipe, without the vegetables, is a must for a homemade Cuban sandwich with sliced pork, ham, Swiss cheese, pickles, and mustard. Sliced pork lunchmeat is hard to come by in grocery stores, and if you can find it, its texture usually bears more resemblance to bologna than pork.

SWEET AND SOUR SPARERIBS

S PARERIBS ARE A CHINESE RESTAURANT favorite of mine but at only 3 or 4 ribs to an order, assembling enough of them for a party would cost an arm and a rib! These have all the tangy and sweet components to re-create my favorite at a fraction of the price.

1. ADD ribs to cooker, then combine remaining ingredients in a mixing bowl, mixing well.

2. POUR sauce mixture over top ribs. Securely lock on cooker's lid, set cooker to HIGH, and cook 10 minutes.

3. LET pressure release naturally 10 minutes before (carefully!) quick releasing remaining pressure and safely removing the lid. Serve as an appetizer, or serve with rice.

SHOPPING LIST

2–4 pounds spareribs, cut into 4 rib pieces

½ onion, diced

¾ cup water

⅔ cup light brown sugar

1 cup ketchup

2 tablespoons vinegar

2 tablespoons orange juice

2 tablespoons soy sauce

PORK

Bob's Tips   Sweet and sour not your thing? Make BBQ Spareribs by replacing everything but the ribs and water with a batch of my Stick to Your Ribs BBQ sauce (recipe page: 187).

ITALIAN SAUSAGE, PEPPERS, AND ONION HOAGIES

HOAGIE, HERO, GRINDER, OR WHATEVER you'd like to call it, this recipe for Italian sausage, peppers, and onions will make your next sandwich worthy of a name with gusto! Though the recipe calls for sweet Italian sausage, try it with hot Italian sausage if you dare. Cook those up on game day for a touchdown every time!

1. ADD oil to pressure cooker, and heat on HIGH or "BROWN" with the lid off.

2. ADD sausages, and sauté until well browned on 2 sides.

3. ADD garlic and about ¼ of the onions, and sauté 1 minute.

4. ADD remaining ingredients. Securely lock on cooker's lid, set cooker to HIGH, and cook 10 minutes.

5. PERFORM a quick release to release cooker's pressure. Safely remove lid, and serve with a slotted spoon into Hoagie rolls. Top with a generous amount of grated Parmesan cheese.

SHOPPING LIST

2 tablespoons olive oil

2 pounds sweet or mild Italian sausage

2 teaspoons minced garlic

2 white onions, peeled, cut in half, and sliced in ½-inch wide strips

1 cup green bell pepper, cored and sliced in ½-inch wide strips

1 cup red bell pepper, cored and sliced in ½-inch wide strips

½ cup dry white wine

1 cup water

1 teaspoon Italian seasoning

½ teaspoon salt

½ teaspoon ground black pepper

6 Hoagie rolls

Parmesan cheese, for garnish

Bob's Tips

Though nothing beats an Italian sausage Hoagie, you can also serve the sausage, peppers, and onions over pasta with red sauce or even alongside roasted potatoes and veggies.

Cooking Times
Veal, Lamb, and Venison

When cooking veal, lamb, and venison, letting the pressure release naturally for 10 minutes is recommended for the most tender meat. However, quick releasing the pressure is recommended for thin cuts of veal. Brown the meat before pressure cooking for best flavor.

VEAL	SIZE	LIQUID	COOK MINUTES	TEMP
ROAST	3–4 pounds	2 cups	45	HIGH
SHANKS	2-inch thick	1½ cups	20	HIGH
STEAKS	½-inch thick	½ cup	5	HIGH
LAMB				
BREAST	2–3 pounds	2 cups	40	HIGH
CHOPS	½-inch thick	½ cup	5	HIGH
CHOPS	1-inch thick	½ cup	12	HIGH
LEG	3–4 pounds	2 cups	40	HIGH
SHANKS	cut in half	1½ cups	25	HIGH
VENISON				
ROAST	4–5 pounds	2 cups	40	HIGH
STEW MEAT	1-inch cubes	1½ cups	12	HIGH

VEAL AND LAMB

Braised Lamb Shanks with Lemon and Mint

EVEN IF YOU HAIL FROM THE HEART OF Scandinavia, you'll be saying "Opa!" when you taste this delicious, traditional Greek pairing of flavors. The sharpness of the lemon and the fresh taste of the mint are perfect complements to the unique flavor of the lamb.

1. HEAT oil in pressure cooker on HIGH or "BROWN" with the lid off, until sizzling.

2. ADD lamb shanks, and brown well on all sides. When almost browned, add garlic to infuse it into the meat.

3. ADD wine, chicken base mixture, tomato paste, sliced lemon, and fresh mint. Securely lock on cooker's lid, set cooker to HIGH, and cook 20 minutes.

4. PERFORM a quick release to release cooker's pressure before safely removing the lid. Add onion, carrots, and celery. Re-secure cooker's lid, set cooker to HIGH, and cook an additional 5 minutes.

5. LET pressure release naturally 10 minutes before quick releasing remaining pressure and safely removing the lid. Salt and pepper to taste. Serve topped with lemon zest and fresh chopped mint.

SHOPPING LIST

2 tablespoons vegetable oil

3 lamb shanks, cut in half, excess fat trimmed off

1 tablespoon minced garlic

1 cup dry white wine

2 teaspoons chicken base (see page: 12) mixed into 2 cups water

3 tablespoons tomato paste

1 lemon, sliced thick

1 tablespoon chopped fresh mint

1 onion, sliced thick

2 carrots, cut into 2-inch lengths

2 stalks celery, cut into 2-inch lengths

Salt and pepper to taste

Zest of 1 lemon, to top

Fresh mint, chopped, to top

 Make sure to ask your butcher to cut the lamb shanks in half; do not attempt to do it yourself! Lamb shoulder can also be used in place of the shanks by cutting the shoulder into 2-inch thick pieces.

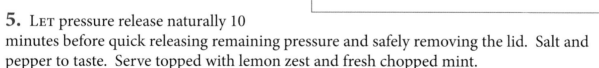

VEAL PARMIGIANA

THIS CLASSIC ITALIAN DISH IS NOT AS crispy in the pressure cooker, but it's so easy and so tender that I absolutely had to include it here. Plus, if veal isn't your thing, this is like two recipes in one, as thin chicken breasts are easily substituted!

SHOPPING LIST

2 tablespoons olive oil

1–2 pounds veal scallopini (about ¼-inch thick)

1 cup Italian bread crumbs

1 (24- to 26-ounce) jar marinara sauce

½ cup dry red wine

½ cup grated Parmesan cheese

1 cup shredded mozzarella cheese, optional

1. POUR olive oil into pressure cooker, and heat on HIGH or "BROWN" with the lid off, until sizzling.

2. DIP veal scallopini in bread crumbs until well coated. Add veal to cooker, browning each piece on both sides.

3. ADD remaining ingredients, except Parmesan and mozzarella cheeses. Securely lock on cooker's lid, set cooker to HIGH, and cook 6 minutes.

4. LET pressure release naturally 5 minutes before quick releasing remaining pressure and safely removing the lid.

5. IMMEDIATELY top with Parmesan and mozzarella cheeses, and gently set lid on top of cooker (no need to lock on or secure) to retain some heat and melt the cheese. Once cheese has melted, serve over pasta with some of the sauce.

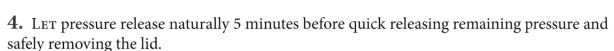

If you would like to brown the cheese, skip the last step in the recipe, and instead top veal with cheese on a sheet pan. Place under your oven's broiler on HIGH, and watch carefully as the cheese will brown VERY fast!

Shown with *Roasted Garlic and Lemon Risotto* (recipe page: **167**)

OSSO BUCO

MOST PEOPLE WOULD NEVER ATTEMPT TO make Osso Buco at home, since it is typically time consuming, and labor intensive. The pressure cooker dramatically changes the cook time of this dish to only 20 minutes.

1. ADD olive oil to pressure cooker, and heat on HIGH or "BROWN" with the lid off. Dip veal shanks in seasoned flour until well coated. Add to cooker, and lightly brown on both sides.

2. ADD garlic, onion, carrots, and celery, and sauté 1 minute before covering with remaining Osso Buco ingredients.

3. SECURELY lock on cooker's lid, set cooker to HIGH, and cook 20 minutes.

4. COMBINE all Gremolata ingredients in a small bowl.

5. WHEN Osso Buco is finished cooking, let pressure release naturally 10 minutes before quick releasing remaining pressure and safely removing the lid. Serve topped with Gremolata.

Bob's Tips

Serve over risotto for true Italian presentation. Osso Buco is one of the few dishes Italians don't serve the meat and starch as separate courses!

SHOPPING LIST

OSSO BUCO

3 tablespoons olive oil

3–4 pounds veal shanks, 4 shanks cut 1–1½ inches thick

1 cup flour, mixed with ½ teaspoon salt and ½ teaspoon pepper

1 red onion, chopped

2 tablespoons minced garlic

2 carrots, cut into ¼-inch discs

2 stalks celery, chopped

1 teaspoon chicken base (see page: 12) mixed into ½ cup water

1 cup white wine

1 (14- to 16-ounce) can diced tomatoes

2 tablespoons tomato paste

2 teaspoons Italian seasoning

Salt and pepper to taste

GREMOLATA

1 tablespoon minced garlic

½ cup chopped fresh parsley

Zest of 1 lemon

¼ teaspoon salt

Prep Time	Cook Time	Serves	Temperature
15 MINS	5 MINS	SIX	HIGH

OLIVE INFUSED LAMB CHOPS WITH RED WINE

THIS DISH SHOUTS OUT SUNSHINE. With very little effort you can picture yourself sitting on a terrace overlooking the Mediterranean, sharing a meal with friends. Have a glass of wine while you're cooking, and enjoy the feel of the sun on your face.

1. COMBINE all ingredients, except lamb chops, in a blender or food processor, and blend until a smooth marinade is formed.

2. COVER lamb chops with marinade in a large bowl or food storage container. Cover, and refrigerate at least 1 hour before cooking.

SHOPPING LIST

2 tablespoons olive oil

¼ cup pitted black olives

2 tablespoons minced garlic

1 teaspoon dried rosemary

1 teaspoon dried oregano

1 cup dry red wine

6 lamb chops, ½ inch thick, trimmed of excess fat

3. HEAT pressure cooker on HIGH or "BROWN" with the lid off, and add 2 tablespoons marinade.

4. ADD lamb chops to cooker, and lightly brown on both sides, 2–3 minutes.

5. COVER chops with remaining marinade. Securely lock on cooker's lid, set cooker to HIGH, and cook 5 minutes.

6. LET pressure release naturally 10 minutes before quick releasing remaining pressure and safely removing the lid. Remove chops to rest under aluminum foil for 5 minutes before serving. Serve with a spoonful of cooking liquid poured over top to moisten.

Lighter side dishes go best with the strong flavors of the olive and wine. Steamed vegetables and parsley or mashed potatoes would make a wonderful meal.

VEAL/LAMB

VEAL FRANCAISE

THIS RECIPE FOR VEAL IN A LEMON BUTTER sauce is French cooking at its most basic. If I've learned anything, it's that with a little butter, you too can be a French chef. If you're a margarine person, however, I don't have anything clever to say about that!

1. POUR olive oil, butter, and garlic into pressure cooker, and heat on HIGH or "BROWN" with the lid off, until sizzling.

2. DIP veal scallopini in seasoned flour, coating well. Add veal to cooker, browning each piece on both sides before adding in remaining ingredients, except cornstarch and garnish.

3. SECURELY lock on cooker's lid, set cooker to HIGH, and cook 6 minutes.

4. LET pressure release naturally 5 minutes before quick releasing remaining pressure and safely removing the lid.

SHOPPING LIST

1 tablespoon olive oil

3 tablespoons butter or margarine

1–2 pounds veal scallopini (about ¼-inch thick)

1 cup flour, mixed with pinches of salt and pepper

1 tablespoon minced garlic

½ teaspoon chicken base (see page: 12) mixed into ½ cup water

½ cup dry white wine

¼ cup lemon juice

1 tablespoon cornstarch, optional

Salt and pepper to taste

1 lemon, sliced thin, for garnish

5. SALT and pepper to taste, and serve with pasta or potatoes, drizzled with cooking liquid and garnished with lemon. To thicken cooking liquid: Remove veal from cooker, setting aside under foil to keep warm. Combine 1 tablespoon cornstarch with 2 tablespoons water in a small dish, and stir into cooker on HIGH or "BROWN" with lid off, simmering until thick. Return veal to cooker to coat well before serving.

Bob's Tips

If your grocery store does not sell thinly sliced veal scallopini, purchase veal cutlets and pound down to ¼ inch thick; sandwich the cutlets between two sheets of plastic wrap on a sturdy cutting board, and hammer with a mallet.

COOKING TIMES
SEAFOOD

WHEN COOKING SEAFOOD, quick releasing the pressure is a must. Thicker fillets of fish and larger shrimp or scallops are recommended, as seafood is very delicate. Cooking on a metal pressure cooker rack is also recommended. Add 1 minute to the cooking times if using frozen.

SEAFOOD	LIQUID	COOK MINUTES	TEMP
CLAMS	½ cup	5	HIGH
COD	½ cup	4	HIGH
CRAB LEGS, SMALL	½ cup	2	HIGH
LOBSTER TAIL, ½ POUND	½ cup	5	HIGH
MUSSELS	½ cup	3	HIGH
SALMON	½ cup	6	HIGH
SCALLOPS, BAY	½ cup	1	HIGH
SCALLOPS, SEA	½ cup	2	HIGH
SHRIMP	½ cup	2	HIGH

SEAFOOD

PAELLA

MUCH LIKE A STEW OR A GUMBO, THIS Spanish rice dish has many variations. This variation is known as a mixed Paella, as it includes chicken, sausage, and seafood.

1. SOAK saffron in 2 tablespoons warm water in a small dish at least 20 minutes.

2. ADD olive oil, garlic, and sausage to cooker, and cook on HIGH or "BROWN" with lid off, breaking up sausage into small pieces with a spatula. Add chicken, onion, and rice; stir until rice is fully coated with oil and chicken begins to turn white.

3. TOP with saffron and remaining ingredients, except shrimp, scallops, bell pepper, and parsley. Securely lock on lid, set cooker to HIGH, and cook 8 minutes.

4. PERFORM a quick release to release pressure before safely removing the lid. Stir in shrimp, scallops, and bell pepper, then re-secure lid, set cooker to HIGH, and cook 2 additional minutes.

5. PERFORM a quick release to release pressure before safely removing the lid. Salt and pepper to taste, and garnish with parsley before serving.

SHOPPING LIST

5 strands saffron

3 tablespoons olive oil

1 tablespoon minced garlic

½ pound chorizo sausage

1 pound boneless, skinless chicken thighs, each thigh cut into 3 strips

1 onion, diced

2 cups short grain white rice, uncooked

1 can stewed tomatoes, drained well

4 teaspoons chicken base (see page: 12) mixed into 4 cups water

½ cup dry white wine

Zest of 1 lemon

1 bay leaf

½ pound shrimp, shelled and deveined

½ pound scallops

1 red bell pepper, diced

Salt and pepper to taste

Parsley, for garnish

SEAFOOD

Bob's Tips

Many variations of Paella include mussels, but with this many other ingredients involved, mussels may not fit in your pressure cooker. You can always cook them separately and add them to the dish at the end. Scrub and de-beard them well, then simmer with 1½ cups white wine for 5 minutes, until they open.

HONEY PECAN SALMON STEAKS

PECANS ARE THE ONLY THING I LOVE MORE on salmon than honey, but with this recipe I get them both! Thicker than a glaze, the topping on these thick-cut salmon steaks is unbelievably easy to put together, and unendingly brag-worthy.

1. ADD water to pressure cooker, and place salmon steaks over top.

2. COMBINE remaining ingredients in a small bowl, then spoon the mixture equally across the tops of all 4 salmon steaks.

3. SECURELY lock on cooker's lid, set cooker to HIGH, and cook 6 minutes.

4. PERFORM a quick release to release cooker's pressure, and safely remove lid. Use a spatula to serve immediately.

SEAFOOD

SHOPPING LIST

½ cup water

4 thick-cut salmon steaks, about 1 inch thick

2 tablespoons butter, melted

1 tablespoon honey

3 tablespoons whole grain mustard

¼ cup finely chopped pecans

2 teaspoons light brown sugar

2 teaspoons parsley flakes

Salt and pepper to taste

Bob's Tips

I like to serve this with sautéed carrots and rice pilaf or jasmine rice, but it would also go well with fingerling or new potatoes.

SHRIMP SCAMPI

THIS GRATIFYING OVERLOAD OF GARLIC, butter, and wine is one of those recipes that is so popular it needs no introduction. Okay, enjoy.

1. ADD all ingredients to pressure cooker. Securely lock on the lid, set cooker to HIGH, and cook 2 minutes.

2. PERFORM a quick release to release cooker's pressure, and safely remove lid. Salt and pepper to taste.

3. SERVE over linguine or your favorite pasta, topped with shredded Parmesan cheese.

SHOPPING LIST

1 pound shrimp, peeled and deveined

4 tablespoons butter or margarine

2 tablespoons minced garlic

¾ cup dry white wine

1 tablespoon lemon juice

¼ teaspoon paprika

2 teaspoons chopped parsley

Salt and pepper to taste

Shredded Parmesan cheese, for garnish

SEAFOOD

Bob's Tips

It should go without saying that a recipe is only the sum of its ingredients. A good quality white wine can make all the difference in a recipe like this. Somebody once said to me, "If you wouldn't drink it, don't cook with it!," and I've adhered to that ever since. The good thing is that there are some very good wines in the $7–$10 range these days.

MEDITERRANEAN SCALLOPS

THIS SCALLOP DISH IS A LIGHT AND delicious taste of Italy and Greece effortlessly delivered to your table in only 12 minutes. With Roma tomatoes and feta cheese, I'll let you figure out which country each influence is from!

1. RINSE scallops well.

2. ADD tomatoes to pressure cooker, then layer scallops over top.

3. COVER with remaining ingredients, except feta cheese. Securely lock on cooker's lid, set cooker to HIGH, and cook 2 minutes.

4. PERFORM a quick release to release cooker's pressure, and safely remove the lid. Salt and pepper to taste. Serve over your favorite pasta, topped with feta cheese.

SHOPPING LIST

1 pound scallops

6 Roma or plum tomatoes, chopped large

2 tablespoons olive oil

2 tablespoons butter or margarine

2 teaspoons minced garlic

½ red onion, diced

½ cup dry white wine

1 tablespoon lemon juice

1 teaspoon oregano

½ cup feta cheese

Salt and pepper to taste

SEAFOOD

Bob's Tips

This recipe goes great with delicate pasta like angel hair or even orzo. If you'd prefer, shrimp can easily be substituted in place of the scallops—or use ¾ pound of each for a Mediterranean Seafood Pasta because two is always better than one!

MUSSELS FRA DIAVOLO

THIS ITALIAN DISH OF MUSSELS, STEWED tomatoes, and a little bit of heat is the perfect way to spice up your night. No need to wait for a special occasion to give these a try—though you may have to wait until you've built up the courage!

1. RINSE and de-beard mussels.

2. ADD all ingredients to pressure cooker, except mussels, and stir well.

3. ADD mussels on top of mixture in cooker. Securely lock on cooker's lid, set cooker to HIGH, and cook 3 minutes.

4. PERFORM a quick release to release cooker's pressure, and safely remove the lid. Salt and pepper to taste. Serve over your favorite pasta, garnished with additional fresh parsley.

SHOPPING LIST

2 pounds mussels

2 tablespoons olive oil

1 onion, chopped

2 teaspoons minced garlic

1 (14- to 16-ounce) can diced tomatoes

½ cup dry white wine

3 tablespoons tomato paste

1 teaspoon Italian seasoning

½ teaspoon crushed red pepper

1 tablespoon chopped fresh parsley

Salt and pepper to taste

Bob's Tips   For the true, and truly spicy, effect of a Fra Diavolo, throw in a fresh chili pepper or two.

CHEESY ONE POT TUNA "CASSEROLE"

THIS DISH IS ANOTHER CLASSIC AMERICAN family-style recipe that everyone in your house will love. It reminds me of a certain helpful boxed dinner, but why make dinner from a box when you can make it fresh? Try this recipe for yourself, and I am sure you'll be asking the same thing!

1. ADD egg noodles, chicken base mixture, tuna, bell pepper, and butter to cooker. Securely lock on lid, set cooker to HIGH, and cook 4 minutes.

2. PERFORM a quick release to release cooker's pressure. Safely remove lid, and slowly stir in Parmesan cheese, Cheddar cheese, cream cheese, and peas until cheeses are melted and creamy. Salt and pepper to taste, and serve immediately, topped with cracker crumbs.

SHOPPING LIST

3 cups egg noodles, uncooked

3 teaspoons chicken base (see page: 12) mixed into 3 cups water

2 cans white tuna, drained well

½ red bell pepper, finely diced

2 tablespoons butter or margarine

1 tablespoon grated Parmesan cheese

1 cup shredded sharp Cheddar cheese

2 ounces cream cheese (¼ regular-size brick)

1 cup frozen peas, thawed

Salt and pepper to taste

1 cup crumbled crackers (Ritz suggested)

SEAFOOD

Bob's Tips

For something a little different, try topping with sour cream and onion potato chips (crumbled) instead of crackers.

COOKING TIMES
BEANS AND LEGUMES

WHEN COOKING BEANS AND LEGUMES, do not fill your pressure cooker more than half full. All cooking times listed are for unsoaked beans. When cooking beans, add enough water to cover the beans plus 2 tablespoons vegetable oil to prevent them from foaming. For firm beans, quick release the pressure. For soft, let the pressure release naturally.

BEANS	COOK MINUTES	TEMP
BLACK BEANS	20	HIGH
BLACK-EYED PEAS	8	HIGH
CANNELLINI	35	HIGH
GARBANZO (CHICKPEAS)	35	HIGH
GREAT NORTHERN	25	HIGH
KIDNEY OR PINTO	22	HIGH
LENTILS, GREEN	8	HIGH
LENTILS, RED OR YELLOW	4	HIGH
LIMA	12	HIGH
NAVY	20	HIGH
PEANUTS, RAW	60	HIGH
SOY	28	HIGH
SPLIT PEAS	6	HIGH

Beans and Legumes

BLACK-EYED PEA SALAD

THIS CHILLED BLACK-EYED PEA SALAD is a refreshing alternative to an Italian pasta salad for your next party or family get together. The soft black-eyed peas are complemented perfectly by the crunchy raw bell pepper and smoky bacon. It's a simple, yet surprisingly new and unique picnic dish that is all prepped and ready to impress in minutes!

1. COMBINE black-eyed peas, oil, and spices in pressure cooker. Add enough water to cover beans.

2. SECURELY lock on cooker's lid, set cooker to HIGH, and cook 9 minutes.

3. PERFORM a quick release, safely remove lid, and test one of the peas for doneness. Peas should be firm enough to hold up to being mixed into the salad without turning into a mash. If too firm for your taste, re-secure lid, and cook on HIGH an additional 2 minutes.

4. DRAIN black-eyed peas into colander, and cool them down by running cold water over them. Combine with all Salad ingredients, stirring well.

SHOPPING LIST

BLACK-EYED PEAS

2 cups black-eyed peas

2 tablespoons vegetable oil, to prevent foaming

½ teaspoon garlic powder

½ teaspoon onion powder

½ teaspoon Italian seasoning

¼ teaspoon ground black pepper

SALAD

1 green bell pepper, cored and finely diced

1 yellow bell pepper, cored and finely diced

½ cup cooked bacon pieces (can buy pre-cooked in salad dressing section)

1 cup robust Italian salad dressing

2 tablespoons mayonnaise

½ teaspoon ground black pepper

Fresh parsley, for garnish

BEANS

5. COVER, and refrigerate at least 2 hours before serving.

Bob's Tips

Though you can serve this as soon as it's chilled (or even as a warm salad), letting the salad marinate overnight really brings the flavors together. I look for a good Italian dressing with plenty of spices and minced garlic at the bottom of the bottle for the best (and fastest) marinade.

ONE POT BLACK BEANS AND RICE

THIS TAKE ON A CUBAN CLASSIC IS ALL mixed up…literally. So simple, yet layered with flavors; serve this on its own as a vegetarian entrée, or grill up some chicken skewers to lie over top. Throw a few sliced plantains on the grill for as close to an authentic Cuban meal as a farm boy like me knows anything about!

1. ADD olive oil, onion, and bell pepper to pressure cooker, and heat on HIGH or "BROWN" with the lid off for 5 minutes, until onions are almost translucent. Turn off.

2. COVER with remaining ingredients, except water and rice, and stir well to combine. Pat the mixture down softly with a spoon to even it out.

3. SLOWLY pour water over top the bean mixture without stirring. Then pour rice over top everything.

4. SECURELY lock on cooker's lid, set cooker to HIGH, and cook 4 minutes.

SHOPPING LIST

2 tablespoons olive oil

½ onion, chopped

½ green bell pepper, diced

1 (14- to 16-ounce) can black beans, with liquid

1 teaspoon oregano

¼ teaspoon sugar

2 teaspoons cider vinegar

½ teaspoon chicken base (see page: 12) mixed into ½ cup water

¼ teaspoon cumin

¼ teaspoon garlic powder

2½ cups water

1½ cups long grain white rice, uncooked

Salt and pepper to taste

5. LET pressure release naturally 5 minutes before quick releasing remaining pressure and safely removing the lid. Let cool 5 minutes for rice to fluff up before serving.

Bob's Tips

If you'd prefer to keep things separate—serving the beans over the rice—follow the first two steps on the stove over medium-high heat as you cook the water and rice in the pressure cooker on HIGH for 4 minutes. Once beans are bubbling, lower heat to a simmer until the rice is ready.

BEANS

HONEY BAKED BEANS

THIS RECIPE FOR A BBQ AND PICNIC STAPLE uses honey instead of the molasses in more traditional baked beans. Just don't leave a batch lying around or a bee or two might bring the whole thing to their queen, bean by bean. Then they'd come for the burgers! This would probably not happen.

1. ADD beans and vegetable oil to pressure cooker, and cover with water up to at least 1½ inches above beans. Securely lock on cooker's lid, set cooker to HIGH, and cook 10 minutes.

2. PERFORM a quick release to release cooker's pressure, and safely remove lid. Drain beans.

SHOPPING LIST

1 pound dried white navy beans, soaked for 6 hours

2 tablespoons vegetable oil

Water to cover beans

2 tablespoons ketchup

¼ cup honey

½ cup light brown sugar

½ teaspoon garlic powder

½ teaspoon onion powder

1 cup water

3. RETURN beans to cooker, cover with ketchup, honey, brown sugar, garlic powder, onion powder, and 1 cup water, and stir well. Re-lock on cooker's lid, set cooker to HIGH, and cook 3 additional minutes.

4. LET pressure release naturally 15 minutes before quick releasing any remaining pressure, safely removing the lid, and serving.

Replace the ketchup with a good BBQ sauce for beans with a bit more bang. Throw ¼ cup chopped raw bacon in with the beans in step 1 of the cooking process for something even better! Add sliced hot dogs in step 3 for that "beanie" childhood favorite with a rhyming name!

BEANS

SPINACH AND ARTICHOKE HUMMUS

WHEN TRADITIONAL HUMMUS GETS A little ho-hum, dip into this new take on two classics! Is it hummus? Is it spinach and artichoke dip? It's all the creaminess of both, but surprisingly different in a very good way!

1. COMBINE chickpeas, water, oil, and salt in pressure cooker. Securely lock on cooker's lid, set cooker to HIGH, and cook 35 minutes.

2. LET pressure release naturally before safely removing the lid. Drain chickpeas into a colander. Cool chickpeas to room temperature by running under cold water.

3. RESERVE ¼ jar artichoke hearts and ½ artichoke marinade; pour remaining artichokes and marinade into a blender with chickpeas, lemon juice, garlic, and Parmesan cheese.

SHOPPING LIST

CHICKPEAS

3 cups dried chickpeas

2 quarts water, or enough to cover chickpeas by 2 inches

2 tablespoons vegetable oil, to prevent foaming

½ teaspoon salt

HUMMUS

1 (12- to 14-ounce) jar marinated artichoke hearts

1 tablespoon lemon juice

1 tablespoon minced garlic

½ cup grated or shredded Parmesan cheese

Salt and pepper to taste

1 cup fresh spinach leaves

4. BLEND on LOW until smooth, but still thick. Add reserved artichoke marinade until you've reached desired texture. Season to taste.

5. ADD reserved artichoke hearts and spinach to blender, and pulse a few seconds until spinach is broken up. Serve immediately, topped with more grated Parmesan cheese for garnish.

Though this isn't exactly your traditional hummus, feel free to serve it the traditional way with warm pita bread. I prefer grilling pita bread on an indoor grill, grill pan, or Panini press. This is also great as a bruschetta (crusty Italian bread, thinly sliced, and grilled) topping.

BEANS

CURRIED LENTILS

LENTILS ARE AN INEXPENSIVE (AND protein packed) legume that don't have a very pronounced flavor. This recipe gets a major boost in the taste department with a good amount of curry. Serve as a vegetarian entrée or as the perfect side for any meal that could use a little pick me up.

1. RINSE lentils in a colander, picking through them to make sure there are no stones or other objects.

2. ADD all ingredients to pressure cooker, and stir. Securely lock on the lid, set cooker to HIGH, and cook 7 minutes.

3. PERFORM a quick release to release cooker's pressure, and safely remove lid. Test lentils for doneness. If not to your liking, re-lock on the lid, and cook on HIGH for an additional 2 minutes. Salt to taste, and serve with a slotted spoon.

SHOPPING LIST

2 cups dried lentils

2 tablespoons vegetable oil

5 teaspoons chicken base (see page: 12) mixed into 5 cups water

1 large onion, chopped

1 tablespoon minced garlic

2 teaspoons curry powder

¼ teaspoon turmeric

Salt to taste

Bob's Tips For a spicier curry, try adding a teaspoon each of chili powder and ground ginger. For even spicier yet, throw in a pinch of cayenne pepper.

BEANS

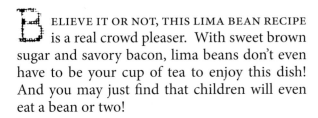

BUTTERY LIMA BEANS WITH SWEET BACON

BELIEVE IT OR NOT, THIS LIMA BEAN RECIPE is a real crowd pleaser. With sweet brown sugar and savory bacon, lima beans don't even have to be your cup of tea to enjoy this dish! And you may just find that children will even eat a bean or two!

1. ADD butter, bacon, and red onion to pressure cooker, and heat on HIGH or "BROWN" with the lid off 3–4 minutes, until onions begin to turn translucent.

2. ADD brown sugar to pot, and stir well.

3. COVER with lima beans and water. Securely lock on cooker's lid, set cooker to HIGH, and cook 8 minutes.

SHOPPING LIST

2 tablespoons butter or margarine

⅔ cup cooked bacon pieces (sold precooked in salad dressing aisle)

½ red onion, diced

¼ cup light brown sugar

1 (16-ounce) bag frozen lima beans

½ cup water

Salt and pepper to taste

BEANS

4. PERFORM a quick release to release cooker's pressure before safely removing the lid. Salt and pepper to taste, and serve.

Bob's Tips

I prefer to make this with the smaller "baby lima beans" but it can be made with any lima bean or butterbean, or pretty much any variety of frozen bean for that matter.

SOUTHERN STYLE BOILED PEANUTS

THESE BOILED PEANUTS ARE A STAPLE IN the South where they are cooked up in copper pots or even giant drums on the side of the road. Cooked in much the same way as a bean, it's an entirely different take on peanuts—soft, salty, and incredibly irresistible. Traditionally, they are boiled in salt water for well over four hours to get to where the pressure cooker takes them in less than one hour!

1. COMBINE raw peanuts, salt, and Cajun Style Spices (if you would like) in pressure cooker, and add enough water to cover peanuts.

2. SECURELY lock on cooker's lid, set cooker to HIGH, and cook 55 minutes.

SHOPPING LIST

1½ pounds (24 ounces) raw peanuts in shell (usually sold in produce section)

1 tablespoon vegetable oil

4 tablespoons salt

CAJUN STYLE SPICES (OPTIONAL)

2 tablespoons Old Bay Seasoning

1 teaspoon garlic powder

1 teaspoon onion powder

1 teaspoon crushed red pepper flakes

3. LET pressure release naturally at least 10 minutes before quick releasing any remaining pressure to safely remove the lid, and serve.

Though they are cooked in salt, boiled peanuts should be stored in their original cooking juice in the refrigerator, and eaten within 3 or 4 days for best texture. I find that they have their best flavor after reheating in the microwave on day two.

BEANS

Cooking Times
Vegetables

When cooking vegetables, quick releasing the pressure is a must. Only let the pressure release naturally if you are planning on puréeing the result into a soup. Use a metal rack or steam basket for the crispest vegetables.

Vegetable	Liquid	Cook Minutes	Temp
Acorn Squash, halved	1 cup	7	low
Artichoke, whole	1 cup	8	high
Asparagus, thick	½ cup	2	low
Beets, ¼-inch slices	½ cup	5	high
Broccoli or Cauliflower	½ cup	2	low
Brussels Sprouts	½ cup	4	low
Butternut Squash, 1-inch chunks	1 cup	4	low
Cabbage, quartered	to cover	3	low
Carrots, baby or chunks	½ cup	4	low
Corn on the Cob	1 cup	2	low
Eggplant, ½-inch chunks	½ cup	3	low
Green Beans	½ cup	2	low
Peas or Zucchini	½ cup	1	low
Potatoes, whole new	1 cup	5	high
Rutabaga, 1-inch chunks	1 cup	5	high

Vegetables and Side Dishes

VEGGIES

RATATOUILLE

THIS IS ANOTHER CLASSIC FRENCH RECIPE with a million possible variations. Though it may seem like a lot of work at first, this is one of the easiest Ratatouilles you'll find, and at only eight minutes under pressure, it's most certainly the fastest. Try slicing the tomatoes, zucchini, squash, and eggplant into discs for something a little bit closer to the ratatouille you may have seen in a certain animated film!

1. ADD olive oil and garlic to pressure cooker, and heat on HIGH or "BROWN" with the lid off, until sizzling.

2. ADD onions, and cook until they begin to sweat.

3. ADD tomato paste, and stir to thin it out. Add remaining ingredients, pouring vegetable broth over top last. Securely lock on cooker's lid, set cooker to LOW, and cook 6 minutes. Then let sit for 6 additional minutes as pressure releases naturally.

4. PERFORM a quick release to release remaining pressure before safely removing the lid. Serve warm with freshly grated, shredded, or shaved Parmesan cheese.

SHOPPING LIST

4 tablespoons olive oil

2 tablespoons minced garlic

1 large onion, quartered, then thinly sliced

2 tablespoons tomato paste

1 eggplant, cut into 1-inch cubes

1 green bell pepper, cut into ½-inch square pieces

1 red bell pepper, cut into ½-inch square pieces

1 large zucchini, chopped large

1 large yellow squash, chopped large

2 tomatoes, chopped large

2 teaspoons Italian seasoning

1 teaspoon salt

½ teaspoon ground black pepper

½ cup vegetable broth

Parmesan cheese, for garnish

VEGGIES

Bob's Tips

There is much debate over when Ratatouille is at its best, either immediately after preparing while some flavors are still separate, or refrigerated overnight when the flavors have melded together. I prefer it immediately because I didn't do all of that chopping to wait until tomorrow!

SWEET RED CABBAGE WITH SOUR APPLE

THIS SIDE DISH IS AS SIMPLE AND QUICK AS it gets. The perfect accompaniment to a pork roast, chops, or even some good barbecue; this recipe is like every great pork side—sauerkraut, coleslaw, and applesauce—all in one.

1. ADD butter to pressure cooker, and heat on HIGH or "BROWN" with the lid off, until sizzling. Add julienned apples, and sauté 2 minutes, stirring frequently.

2. COVER with remaining ingredients, except cabbage, and stir well to combine.

3. ADD cabbage. Securely lock on cooker's lid, set cooker to HIGH, and cook 1 minute.

4. PERFORM a quick release to release cooker's pressure. Safely remove lid, and let cool 5 minutes before serving.

SHOPPING LIST

1 tablespoon butter or margarine

2 green (tart) apples, peeled, quartered, and julienned

4 tablespoons light brown sugar

½ cup red wine vinegar

¼ cup water

¼ teaspoon ground black pepper

1 head red cabbage, quartered, then sliced thin

Bob's Tips

To julienne peeled apples: cut four sides off of the apple as close to the core as you can get. You should be left with a cubed core that you can discard. Lay the four chunks of apple on their flat side, and slice about ⅙ inch thick. Stack slices a few at a time, and slice into ⅙-inch wide sticks.

VEGGIES

HERB "ROASTED" SUMMER SQUASH

WHILE SUMMER SQUASH SUCH AS THE yellow (technically known as crookneck) squash and zucchini used in this recipe are extremely versatile ingredients, I always seem to fall back on this classic recipe. While this recipe would typically be roasted in the oven, the pressure cooker locks all of the flavors in well, and without compromise.

SHOPPING LIST

2 tablespoons olive oil

1 tablespoon minced garlic

1 red onion, quartered, then thinly sliced

2 zucchini, chopped large

2 yellow squash, chopped large

¼ teaspoon dried rosemary

½ teaspoon dried oregano

2 teaspoons parsley flakes

½ teaspoon salt

¼ teaspoon ground black pepper

½ cup water

1. ADD all ingredients, except water, to pressure cooker, and heat on HIGH or "BROWN" with the lid off, until onions cook down considerably, and squash begins to brown.

2. COVER with ½ cup water. Securely lock on cooker's lid, set cooker to LOW, and cook 5 minutes.

3. PERFORM a quick release to release cooker's pressure before safely removing the lid, and serving with your favorite entrée.

VEGGIES

Bob's Tips

Thoroughly scrub squash under running water before chopping. Zucchini especially tends to carry a lot of grit on its rind that isn't always visible to the naked eye.

GREEN BEAN "CASSEROLE"

GREEN BEAN CASSEROLE IS TRADITIONALLY made with a can of condensed cream of mushroom soup. This fresh homemade version is even better, and with the pressure cooker, the only thing condensed is the cooking time!

1. ADD butter, mushrooms, and garlic to pressure cooker, and heat on HIGH or "BROWN" with the lid off, until mushrooms have cooked down, 3–4 minutes.

2. COVER with green beans, broth, bay leaf, and ⅓ French fried onions. Securely lock on cooker's lid, set cooker to LOW, and cook 2 minutes.

3. PERFORM a quick release to release cooker's pressure before safely removing the lid. Use a slotted spoon to transfer green beans to a casserole dish.

4. SET cooker to HIGH or "BROWN" with lid off, and slowly stir in sour cream and cornstarch mixture, simmering until thick. Salt and pepper to taste, then pour thickened sauce over green beans in casserole dish. Top with remaining ⅔ French fried onions, and serve.

SHOPPING LIST

2 tablespoons butter

8 ounces baby bella mushrooms, finely chopped

1 tablespoon minced garlic

1 (16- to 22-ounce) bag frozen whole green beans

½ cup vegetable broth

1 bay leaf

1 (3-ounce) can French fried onions, divided

1 (16-ounce) carton reduced-fat sour cream

1 tablespoon cornstarch, mixed into 1 tablespoon water

Salt and pepper to taste

VEGGIES

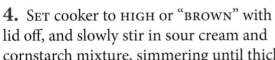

Bob's Tips I like to buy "select" frozen green beans as they are almost indistinguishable from fresh without having to snap fresh beans for fifteen minutes. However, if you prefer, fresh are easily substituted. And if you really want to go homemade—try slicing thin, then sautéing 2 onions in 2 tablespoons butter until well caramelized for an onion topping that makes this an entirely different take on a classic.

CAULIFLOWER WITH CHEESE SAUCE

WHILE I MUST SAY THAT A GOOD CHEESE sauce is a sneaky way to get children to eat their vegetables, I should confess that cauliflower in a cheese sauce is one of my all-time favorite sides, vegetable or not! This recipe is as quick and easy as I've ever made it—oh, and it's just as delicious as ever.

1. ADD all Cauliflower ingredients to pressure cooker. Securely lock on cooker's lid, set cooker to HIGH, and cook 2 minutes.

2. PERFORM a quick release to release cooker's pressure, and safely remove lid

3. GRADUALLY add Cheese Sauce ingredients, stirring until melted and creamy. Salt and pepper to taste, and serve immediately.

SHOPPING LIST

CAULIFLOWER

1 head cauliflower, florets separated

1½ teaspoons chicken base (see page: 12) mixed into 1½ cups water

1 tablespoon butter or margarine

1 tablespoon grated Parmesan cheese

¼ teaspoon onion powder

CHEESE SAUCE

1 cup shredded sharp Cheddar cheese

2 ounces cream cheese (¼ of a regular-size brick)

Salt and pepper to taste

While the cauliflower holds up better to pressure cooking, broccoli florets can easily be substituted in this recipe, or even half cauliflower and half broccoli. Be careful when stirring in the cheese, as broccoli florets break up much easier, and you don't want to end up with broccoli and cheese soup!

VEGGIES

SKILLET RED BLISS POTATOES

THIS IS A PERFECT SIDE DISH TO SERVE AT a Sunday brunch for friends, maybe as an accompaniment to grilled salmon and asparagus. If you don't eat a meal like that outside on a picnic table under a shade tree, you don't know what you're missing.

SHOPPING LIST

8 red bliss potatoes, cut in half

1 cup vegetable broth

1 tablespoon olive oil

2 tablespoons butter

1 teaspoon minced garlic

1 tablespoon parsley flakes

Salt and pepper to taste

1. ADD vegetable broth to pressure cooker. For best results and firmer potatoes, position a steaming rack over broth.

2. PLACE potatoes into broth or onto steaming rack. Securely lock on cooker's lid, set cooker to HIGH, and cook 5 minutes.

3. PERFORM a quick release to release cooker's pressure, and safely remove lid. Drain potatoes into a colander.

4. ADD olive oil, butter, and garlic to cooker, and heat on HIGH or "BROWN" with lid off, until sizzling.

5. RETURN potatoes to cooker, with as many cut-side down as possible, to brown. Brown the cut, flat side of potatoes extremely well, until crispy. Add parsley and salt and pepper to taste before serving.

Bob's Tips

Add in a teaspoon of your favorite dried herb for "roasted" potatoes to match whichever dish you may be serving. Rosemary for beef. Marjoram for chicken. Oregano, thyme, or dill…the possibilities are endless!

VEGGIES

REDSKIN POTATO SALAD WITH DILL

W HETHER YOU PREFER TRADITIONAL OR German style potato salad, this secret recipe of mine has you covered. It's a true original, with the fresh crunch of diced cucumber in place of traditional celery. Cucumbers and dill, I wonder where I got that idea?

1. ADD vegetable broth to pressure cooker. For best results and firmer potatoes, position a steaming rack over broth.

2. PLACE cubed potatoes into broth or onto steaming rack, securely lock on cooker's lid, set cooker to HIGH, and cook 2 minutes.

3. PERFORM a quick release, safely remove lid, and drain potatoes into a colander. Run cold water over them to cool them down to room temperature.

SHOPPING LIST

POTATOES

6 red potatoes (about 2 pounds), cut into ½-inch cubes

1 cup vegetable broth

SALAD

½ onion, diced small

1 small cucumber, chopped small

½ cup mayonnaise

½ cup sour cream

2 tablespoons white vinegar

2 tablespoons fresh dill, chopped

½ teaspoon garlic powder

Salt and pepper to taste

4. COMBINE all Salad ingredients and fold Potatoes in slowly, being careful not to mash them.

5. SALT and pepper to taste, then cover, and refrigerate at least 2 hours before serving.

Though you can serve this as soon as it's chilled (or even as a warm salad), the longer you let the salad marinate, the better. Try adding a tablespoon of sweet relish for a sweet contrast to this savory salad. When sweet and salty go head to head, you can do no wrong!

VEGGIES

MAPLE BUTTER GLAZED CARROTS

Anytime you can make a vegetable taste like dessert and get away with it, you've got a winner. Adults will appreciate the subtlety of the maple and cinnamon; children will simply ask for more.

1. ADD all ingredients, except maple syrup and cornstarch mixture, to pressure cooker. Securely lock on cooker's lid, set cooker to HIGH, and cook 2 minutes.

2. PERFORM a quick release to release cooker's pressure, and safely remove lid.

3. SET cooker to HIGH or "BROWN" with the lid off, and slowly stir in maple syrup and cornstarch mixture, stirring until liquid is thick enough to thoroughly coat carrots. Serve immediately.

SHOPPING LIST

2 tablespoons butter or margarine

3 cups baby carrots

½ cup water

1 tablespoon light brown sugar

½ teaspoon salt

¼ teaspoon cinnamon

¼ cup maple syrup

2 teaspoons cornstarch, mixed into 1 tablespoon water

Bob's Tips

Though baby carrots are easiest with no need to peel, you can use 3 cups sliced carrots. Be sure to slice the carrots thick, at least ¼ of an inch to hold up best under pressure.

VEGGIES

HERBED GREEN BEANS, CARROTS, AND CRANBERRIES

THERE IS NO NEED TO LET YOUR sides sit under aluminum foil to keep warm when you can cook up this holiday hit in only two minutes! Prepare ingredients in the pressure cooker's removable pot (or cooker itself for stovetop cookers) in advance, and refrigerate, covered, until the rest of the meal is nearly ready, and you're set to cook them up fresh, fast, and just in time!

1. ADD all ingredients, except dried cranberries, to pressure cooker, and stir.

2. SECURELY lock on cooker's lid, set cooker to LOW, and cook 2 minutes.

3. PERFORM a quick release to release cooker's pressure before safely removing the lid. Stir in dried cranberries, then salt and pepper to taste.

4. LET mixture rest 2–3 minutes as cranberries soften. Serve with a slotted spoon.

SHOPPING LIST

3 tablespoons butter

1 tablespoon minced garlic

1 (16- to 22-ounce) bag frozen whole green beans

1½ cups peeled and julienned carrots

½ cup vegetable broth

1 teaspoon Italian seasoning

1 tablespoon parsley flakes

½ teaspoon onion powder

½ cup dried cranberries (such as Craisins)

Salt and pepper to taste

VEGGIES

Bob's Tips

To julienne carrots: peel and cut in half. Lay halves down on their flat side, and slice lengthwise into slices about ⅛ inch thick. Stack slices a few at a time, and slice into ⅛-inch wide sticks.

"KETTLE" SWEET CORN ON THE COB

THIS RECIPE FOR CORN ON THE COB REMINDS me of the salty/sweet carnival-style kettle corn that seems to be everywhere these days! We've all had that great ear of corn that was as sweet as candy, but we can't always get that from our local grocery store, so the added sugar here, infused at high pressure, guarantees greatness!

1. ADD water and sugar to pressure cooker, then position a rack over water.

2. PLACE ears of corn on rack as separated from each other as you have room for. (It's okay if they have to overlap.)

3. CUT butter into 4 equal pads, and place 1 on each ear of corn.

4. GENEROUSLY sprinkle each ear of corn with salt.

5. SECURELY lock on cooker's lid, set cooker to HIGH, and cook 3 minutes.

6. PERFORM a quick release to release cooker's pressure. Safely remove lid, and serve.

SHOPPING LIST

1 cup water

¼ cup sugar

4 ears fresh corn, husked

2 tablespoons butter or margarine

1 teaspoon salt

VEGGIES

Bob's Tips

Though you add butter before cooking, when corn on the cob is on the table, it's always a good idea to have more butter and salt nearby!

LOADED SCALLOPED POTATOES

THIS IS ONE OF THOSE FLAVORS YOU GET A craving for, and you can't rest until you get it. Fortunately, this recipe makes it simple to satisfy your basic human need for cheese and bacon without having to find a restaurant that still has potato skins on the menu.

1. ADD sliced potatoes, chicken base mixed with water, and bacon pieces to pressure cooker. Securely lock on the lid, set cooker to HIGH, and cook 2 minutes.

2. PERFORM a quick release to release cooker's pressure. Safely remove lid, and slowly stir in Cheddar and cream cheeses until melted and creamy. Salt and pepper to taste, and serve immediately.

SHOPPING LIST

6 redskin potatoes, sliced into ⅛-inch slices

1 teaspoon chicken base (see page: 12) mixed into 1 cup water

½ cup cooked bacon pieces (can be purchased in salad dressing aisle)

½ cup shredded sharp Cheddar cheese

2 ounces cream cheese (¼ regular-size brick)

Salt and pepper to taste

VEGGIES

Try substituting diced ham in place of the bacon pieces, and adding chopped broccoli florets during the first step of cooking to make a two-minute potato casserole dinner!

CANDIED SWEET POTATOES WITH PECANS

THIS SIDE DISH IS LIKE A LITTLE BIT OF dessert smack dab in the middle of dinner. It's like maple syrup and sweet potatoes were meant to be together, then the pecan came along and created a dish fit for any holiday—or just any day at all.

SHOPPING LIST

3 sweet potatoes, cut into ¾-inch slices, then cubed

2 tablespoons cornstarch

1 cup water

¼ cup sugar

¼ cup light brown sugar

¼ cup maple syrup

2 tablespoons butter or margarine

½ cup chopped pecans

1. Toss cubed sweet potatoes in cornstarch until evenly coated (shaking in a plastic zipper bag works best).

2. PLACE coated potatoes in pressure cooker, cover with remaining ingredients, except pecans, and stir.

3. SECURELY lock on cooker's lid, set cooker to HIGH, and cook 4 minutes.

4. PERFORM a quick release to release cooker's pressure. Safely remove lid, and stir in chopped pecans before serving.

Transfer the potatoes into a casserole dish, top with a layer of marshmallows, and place under the broiler until the marshmallows begin to brown, and you've got the fastest sweet potato casserole you've ever made!

VEGGIES

HOMINY BREAKFAST HASH WITH HAM

HOMINY IS AN ALL TOO OFTEN OVERLOOKED side dish, and when it comes to pressure cookers, breakfast is an all too often overlooked meal. Hominy's dried, then soaked corn kernels may not seem like it at first, but do make the perfect accompaniment to an egg breakfast, as they're most similar in taste and texture to southern grits. This hominy hash with ham is a simple and quick way to kick off your day!

1. BREAK apart any clumps of hominy, and add to cooker.

2. COVER with remaining ingredients, except chives, Colby-Jack cheese, and eggs. Securely lock on cooker's lid, set cooker to HIGH, and cook 2 minutes.

3. LET pressure release naturally 5 minutes before quick releasing remaining pressure and safely removing the lid. Stir in chopped chives, and plate each serving topped with shredded Colby-Jack cheese and an egg cooked sunny side up or over easy.

SHOPPING LIST

1 (14- to 16-ounce) can hominy, drained and rinsed

2 tablespoons butter or margarine

½ teaspoon chicken base (see page: 12) mixed into ½ cup water

½ cup cubed or diced ham (many stores sell ham already cubed or diced)

¼ teaspoon garlic powder

¼ teaspoon onion powder

¼ teaspoon ground black pepper

2 tablespoons chopped chives

½ cup shredded Colby-Jack cheese (optional)

4 large eggs (optional)

VEGGIES

Bob's Tips

Hominy comes in both white and yellow varieties. Both are similar in taste, but I prefer to use white in this recipe for no other reason than it contrasts better with the yellow of the cheese and egg yolk.

Cooking Times
Rice

When cooking rice, do not fill the pressure cooker with any more than 3 cups of dry rice. The following chart lists the ratio for 1 cup of rice to water, but you may double or triple it. Add 2 tablespoons of vegetable oil to prevent foaming. Rice should be rinsed well before cooking, unless you are making short grain risottos or sticky rice. Let the pressure release naturally for fluffy rice. Quick release the pressure for firmer rice. 1 cup dry rice makes around 3 cups cooked.

White Rice	Amount	Liquid	Cook Minutes	Temp
Short Grain	1 cup	2½ cups	7	HIGH
Medium Grain	1 cup	2 cups	6	HIGH
Long Grain	1 cup	1½ cups	4	HIGH
Brown Rice				
Short Grain	1 cup	2 cups	14	HIGH
Medium Grain	1 cup	2 cups	14	HIGH
Long Grain	1 cup	2 cups	10	HIGH
Wild Rice	1 cup	3½ cups	20	HIGH

RICE AND RISOTTO

RICE

ASPARAGUS RISOTTO

BEFORE I STARTED PRESSURE COOKING, risottos were always a mystery that I was sure only world-class chefs could crack. Now, I'm not saying that your pressure cooker gave you a culinary degree, but this rich and creamy Asparagus Risotto will make it taste like it has!

1. TRIM 1½–2 inches off of the bottom, tough end of asparagus, and discard. Trim off asparagus tips 1½ inches from top, and place into a microwave-safe dish with water to cover. Chop remaining asparagus stalks into ½-inch lengths.

2. ADD oil, butter, and garlic to pressure cooker, and heat on HIGH or "BROWN" with lid off, stirring constantly, until sizzling.

3. ADD rice and asparagus stalk pieces (not tips), and stir constantly 1 minute.

SHOPPING LIST

1 pound fresh asparagus

1 tablespoon olive oil

2 tablespoons butter or margarine

1 tablespoon minced garlic

2 cups Arborio or Calrose rice

4 cups vegetable broth

1 cup dry white wine

1 teaspoon lemon juice

¼ cup grated or shredded Parmesan cheese

Salt and pepper to taste

4. ADD remaining ingredients, except Parmesan cheese and asparagus tips. Securely lock on cooker's lid, set cooker to HIGH, and cook 7 minutes.

5. MICROWAVE asparagus tips 2–3 minutes, until tender but not mushy. Drain.

6. WHEN risotto is done, perform a quick release to release pressure. Safely remove lid, stir in Parmesan cheese and asparagus tips. Salt and pepper to taste, and serve immediately.

Bob's Tips

Most asparagus is shrink wrapped in a foam tray, and the easiest way to cut the crunchy and inedible bottoms off is to place the wrapped foam tray on a cutting board, and carefully chop through the entire package and all stalks in one swipe.

RICE

JAMBALAYA

PUT ON SOME ZYDECO TUNES TO PLAY while you cook this Cajun favorite—I *gare-on-tee* that it will taste better. Your body may not be in New Orleans, but that doesn't mean that your heart and mind can't go there!

1. ADD olive oil, garlic, sausage, onion, bell pepper, and celery to pressure cooker, and cook on HIGH or "BROWN" with lid off, until sausage begins to brown, and vegetables begin to sweat.

2. COAT chicken with flour on all sides before adding them to cooker.

3. ADD remaining ingredients, except shrimp and green onion tops, and stir. Securely lock on cooker's lid, set cooker to HIGH, and cook 5 minutes.

4. PERFORM a quick release to release cooker's pressure, and safely remove lid. Switch cooker to HIGH or "BROWN" with the lid off, and stir in shrimp and green onion tops. Stir constantly, until shrimp turn pink, about 3 minutes. Salt and pepper to taste, and serve.

SHOPPING LIST

3 tablespoons olive oil

1 tablespoon minced garlic

½ pound andouille or smoked sausage, cut into ¼-inch slices

1 small onion, chopped large

1 green bell pepper, chopped large

2 stalks celery, chopped

1 pound boneless, skinless chicken thighs, each thigh cut into 3 strips

3 tablespoons flour

1 cup long grain rice, uncooked

2 teaspoons chicken base (see page: 12) mixed into 2 cups water

2 (14- to 16-ounce) cans stewed tomatoes

1 teaspoon thyme

½ teaspoon paprika

¼ teaspoon hot pepper sauce

¼ teaspoon cayenne pepper

1 pound shrimp, peeled and deveined

¼ cup sliced green onion tops

Salt and pepper to taste

Bob's Tips

Jambalaya is probably the most open-ended and versatile dish of the South. Try replacing the sausage with ham, and adding a can of black-eyed peas. And if you really like your spice, try adding fresh sliced jalapeño!

RICE

SEARED CHERRY TOMATO RISOTTO

Though you can pretty much put anything in or on top of a risotto and it will be delicious; there is definitely something special to a tangy/sweet pan-seared cherry tomato. Serve it topped with a juicy grilled steak, and you're in business—the markedly remarkable dinner business.

1. ADD oil, butter, garlic, and 1 cup cherry tomato halves to pressure cooker, and heat on HIGH or "BROWN" with the lid off, stirring constantly, until sizzling.

2. ADD rice, and stir constantly for 1 minute to coat with oil.

3. ADD remaining ingredients, except Parmesan cheese, and stir. Securely lock on cooker's lid, set cooker to HIGH, and cook 7 minutes.

SHOPPING LIST

1 tablespoon olive oil

2 tablespoons butter or margarine

1 tablespoon minced garlic

1½ cups halved cherry tomatoes, divided

2 cups Arborio or Calrose rice

4 teaspoons chicken base (see page: 12) mixed into 4 cups water

1 tablespoon dry red wine

1 tablespoon chopped fresh basil

Salt and pepper to taste

¼ cup shredded Parmesan cheese

4. PERFORM a quick release to release cooker's pressure. Safely remove lid, then salt and pepper to taste. Serve topped with remaining ½ cup cherry tomato halves and shredded Parmesan cheese.

Bob's Tips

Stir in a cup of thawed frozen corn kernels right before serving, letting sit for 2 minutes to warm through for an extra sweet burst of flavor that both complements and contrasts the cherry tomatoes.

RICE

WILD RICE ALMONDINE

THIS WILD RICE DISH ALWAYS REMINDS ME of the holidays! Though the cranberries are optional, I'd highly recommend them if you're cooking poultry. The cranberries and almonds lend a sweet contrast to an otherwise savory side that will all but make the meal!

1. RINSE wild rice thoroughly before adding to pressure cooker.

2. ADD butter, chicken base mixture, garlic powder, and onion powder to cooker with wild rice. Securely lock on the lid, set cooker to HIGH, and cook 20 minutes.

3. PERFORM a quick release to release cooker's pressure. Safely remove lid, and stir in white rice and almond slivers. Lock on cooker's lid, set cooker to HIGH, and cook 5 additional minutes.

SHOPPING LIST

1 cup wild rice

3 tablespoons butter or margarine

3½ teaspoons chicken base (see page: 12) mixed into 3½ cups water

½ teaspoon garlic powder

½ teaspoon onion powder

1 cup long grain white rice

¾ cup blanched almond slivers (sold in baking aisle)

1 tablespoon parsley flakes

½ cup dried cranberries, optional

Salt and pepper to taste

4. LET pressure release naturally 5 minutes before quick releasing remaining pressure and safely removing the lid. Immediately stir in parsley flakes and dried cranberries. Let the rice sit 5 minutes to fluff up as cranberries soften slightly. Salt and pepper to taste, and serve.

Bob's Tips

Wild rice, at 25 minutes, has one of the longest cooking times of any grain in the pressure cooker. When you're cooking a holiday meal for family, you'll surely welcome the extra time to finish cooking other dishes! Also, as it takes longer to cook, it reheats well when prepared in advance.

RICE

APPLE BROWN RICE STUFFING

THIS UNTRADITIONAL STUFFING MADE from brown rice and apple makes a wonderful holiday side dish, or even just the perfect accompaniment to a pork chop dinner. I love pairing apples with poultry or pork, but don't always want a dab of applesauce running all over the plate!

1. PLACE butter, apple, and celery in pressure cooker, and heat on HIGH or "BROWN" with the lid off, stirring constantly for 2–3 minutes, until celery is sweating.

2. ADD rice, and stir constantly for 1 minute to coat with butter.

3. ADD remaining ingredients. Securely lock on cooker's lid, set cooker to HIGH, and cook 12 minutes.

4. LET pressure release naturally 10 minutes before quick releasing remaining pressure and safely removing the lid. Salt and pepper to taste, and serve.

SHOPPING LIST

2 tablespoons butter or margarine

1 apple, peeled, cored, and diced

2 stalks celery, diced

2 cups long grain brown rice, uncooked

2 teaspoons chicken base (see page: 12) mixed into 2 cups water

1 cup apple juice

½ teaspoon poultry seasoning

½ teaspoon dried thyme

½ teaspoon onion powder

⅛ teaspoon cinnamon

Salt and pepper to taste

Bob's Tips

To make this stuffing into a real holiday favorite, try stirring in ½ cup slivered almonds (sold in the baking aisle) and ¼ cup raisins after pressure cooking, and letting sit 2–3 minutes to let the raisins soften slightly before serving.

RICE

PORTABELLA RISOTTO

GRAB A LOAF OF CRUSTY BREAD AND A glass of wine, and enjoy this earthy, satisfying risotto. Though it's hearty enough to eat as a full meal, a great risotto is at its best under lamb chops or veal.

1. PLACE oil, butter, onion, and chopped portabella mushrooms in pressure cooker. Heat on HIGH or "BROWN" with the lid off, stirring constantly for 2 minutes, until mushrooms begin to cook down.

2. ADD rice, and stir constantly for 1 minute to coat with oil.

3. ADD remaining ingredients, except Parmesan cheese. Securely lock on cooker's lid, set cooker to HIGH, and cook 7 minutes.

SHOPPING LIST

1 tablespoon olive oil

2 tablespoons butter or margarine

½ red onion, diced

2 large portabella mushroom caps, chopped

2 cups Arborio or Calrose rice

4 cups vegetable broth

½ cup dry red wine

2 teaspoons dried thyme

¼ cup grated Parmesan cheese

Salt and pepper to taste

4. PERFORM a quick release to release cooker's pressure. Safely remove lid, and stir in Parmesan cheese. Salt and pepper to taste, and serve immediately.

RICE

Bob's Tips

Eight ounces of chopped baby bella mushrooms can easily be substituted for the large portabella mushroom caps without sacrificing any flavor. They seem to go on sale more often than their grown-up counterparts.

RISOTTO WITH GORGONZOLA AND WALNUTS

I CAN'T THINK OF ANY MORE PERFECT complement to a creamy risotto than a good quality, creamy Gorgonzola cheese. Try garnishing this with diced red apples to take this recipe to a whole different place! It's like a warm Waldorf salad and risotto all in one! The sweet apple perfectly contrasts the earthy walnuts and strong Gorgonzola cheese.

1. ADD oil, butter, and diced onion to pressure cooker, and heat on HIGH or "BROWN" with the lid off, stirring constantly, until sizzling.

2. ADD rice, and stir constantly for 1 minute.

3. ADD vegetable broth and white wine; securely lock on cooker's lid, set cooker to HIGH, and cook 7 minutes.

SHOPPING LIST

1 tablespoon olive oil

2 tablespoons butter or margarine

1 onion, diced

2 cups Arborio or Calrose rice

4 cups vegetable broth

1 cup dry white wine

¼ cup grated or shredded Parmesan cheese

6 ounces Gorgonzola cheese crumbles (may substitute any blue cheese)

½ cup chopped walnuts

Salt and pepper to taste

1 red apple, diced, for garnish (optional)

4. PERFORM a quick release to release cooker's pressure. Safely remove lid, stir in Parmesan cheese, Gorgonzola cheese, and chopped walnuts. Salt and pepper to taste, garnish with apple, if desired, and serve immediately.

Bob's Tips

Toasted walnuts work best in this risotto. If you can only find raw walnuts in the store, preheat the oven to 350° and place raw walnuts on a sheet pan in a single layer. Bake 10 minutes, until you can smell the walnuts toasting.

RICE

SESAME FRIED RICE

THE DISTINCT FLAVOR OF SESAME OIL really sets this fried rice apart from the ordinary. No wok necessary, the rice is cooked and then fried right in the pressure cooker, scrambled egg and all. Pictured on page: 82.

SHOPPING LIST

4 tablespoons sesame oil, divided

2 cups long grain white rice, uncooked

2¾ cups water

¼ cup low-sodium soy sauce

2 carrots, peeled and chopped

¾ cup frozen peas

2 large eggs, beaten

1. ADD 2 tablespoons sesame oil, rice, water, soy sauce, and chopped carrots to pressure cooker. Securely lock on cooker's lid, set cooker to HIGH, and cook 4 minutes.

2. LET pressure release naturally 5 minutes before quick releasing remaining pressure and safely removing the lid.

3. DRAIN excess liquid (for firmer rice), or let rice sit 5–10 minutes, until all excess liquid has been absorbed.

4. STIR in remaining 2 tablespoons sesame oil, and set cooker to HIGH or "BROWN" with the lid off.

5. ADD frozen peas, and stir to combine. When cooker has heated up enough to hear the rice sizzling, use a spoon to push the rice from the center outward, up against the walls of cooker, until you've created a hole all the way to the bottom of the pot.

6. POUR beaten eggs into the hole you created in the rice, and let them cook as you would scrambled eggs, breaking them up, and folding them into themselves, until firm. Once firm and scrambled, stir to fully combine with rice, and serve!

Bob's Tips

To substitute long grain brown rice in place of the white, up the cooking time from 4 minutes to 12 minutes.

RICE

ROASTED GARLIC AND LEMON RISOTTO

THIS SAVORY RISOTTO IS A PERFECT complement to chicken, pork, or salmon. The roasted garlic is nutty without being overwhelming, and the acidity of the lemon provides the perfect foil for the creamy richness of the risotto.

1. BLEND roasted garlic, lemon zest, and white wine in a blender or food processor until a paste is formed.

2. PLACE oil, butter, and onion in pressure cooker, and heat on HIGH or "BROWN" with the lid off, stirring constantly, until onions sweat.

3. ADD rice, and stir constantly for 1 minute to coat with oil.

4. ADD garlic paste mixture and vegetable broth, and stir. Securely lock on cooker's lid, set cooker to HIGH, and cook 7 minutes.

SHOPPING LIST

10 cloves garlic, roasted

2 teaspoons lemon zest

½ cup dry white wine

1 tablespoon olive oil

2 tablespoons butter or margarine

½ red onion, diced

2 cups Arborio or Calrose rice

4 cups vegetable broth

¼ cup grated Parmesan cheese

2 tablespoons parsley flakes

Salt and pepper to taste

5. PERFORM a quick release to release cooker's pressure. Safely remove lid, and stir in Parmesan cheese and parsley flakes. Salt and pepper to taste, and serve immediately.

Bob's Tips Nowadays, whole, peeled, and separated garlic cloves are readily available in most grocery stores. They usually come in a plastic jar in the produce section. To roast them: Preheat the oven to 400°, and line a baking sheet with foil. Lay garlic cloves out in a single layer, and cover with another sheet of aluminum foil. Bake for 15–20 minutes, until cloves turn a golden brown.

RICE

Cooking Times
Pasta

WHEN COOKING PASTA, do not fill the pressure cooker with any more than 4 cups dry pasta. Add enough water to cover pasta by at least 3 inches. Add 2 tablespoons of vegetable oil to prevent foaming. Drain after cooking. For couscous, add 1½ cups of liquid for each cup of couscous, and there is no need to drain. When cooking any pasta, quick releasing the pressure is a must.

Pasta	Cook Minutes	Temp
Farfalle	5	HIGH
Couscous	2	HIGH
Elbows	6	HIGH
Fettuccine	6	HIGH
Linguine	6	HIGH
Orzo	4	HIGH
Penne	7	HIGH
Rotini	6	HIGH
Tortellini, dried	5	HIGH
Tortellini, fresh	3	HIGH

PASTA

MOST EXCELLENT MACARONI AND CHEESE

TAKING ON THE KING OF ALL COMFORT foods was no easy task for me and my pressure cooker. It took many trials and far too many errors to come out with a real winner of a dinner, but I think I've done it! All the creaminess you'd expect in under the time it used to take to boil pasta. It's proof positive that comfort food only needs to taste like you spent all day in the kitchen.

1. ADD all Macaroni ingredients to pressure cooker. Securely lock on cooker's lid, set cooker to HIGH, and cook 6 minutes.

2. PERFORM a quick release to release cooker's pressure. Safely remove lid, and slowly stir in all Cheese ingredients until melted and creamy. Serve immediately.

SHOPPING LIST

MACARONI

2½ cups elbow macaroni

2 teaspoons chicken base (see page: 12) mixed into 2 cups water

1 cup water

2 tablespoons butter or margarine

1 tablespoon grated Parmesan cheese

CHEESE

2 cups shredded sharp Cheddar cheese

2 ounces cream cheese (¼ regular-size brick)

1 teaspoon yellow mustard

Bob's Tips

I won't lie; sometimes I like to make this recipe with 2 cups of pasteurized cheese, such as Velveeta, instead of the Cheddar and cream cheeses. For me, it's just as much a comfort food as macaroni and cheese itself! You can also run frozen broccoli florets under hot water for 3 minutes, until they've completely thawed, and then toss into the finished macaroni with cubed ham for a no-bake casserole in minutes!

PASTA

ORZO PRIMAVERA

THIS LIGHT AND REFRESHING PASTA DISH with a bevy of beautiful, brightly colored vegetables may just remind you of spring. It's no coincidence, as that's where Primavera gets its name! The small, almost rice-size orzo pasta is yet another breath of fresh air when you're tired of ordinary rice or pasta.

1. ADD oil, butter, minced garlic, and onion to pressure cooker, and heat on HIGH or "BROWN" with the lid off, stirring constantly, until sizzling.

2. COVER with remaining ingredients, except Parmesan cheese. Securely lock on cooker's lid, set cooker to HIGH, and cook 4 minutes.

3. PERFORM a quick release to release cooker's pressure. Safely remove lid, and stir in Parmesan cheese. Salt and pepper to taste, and serve using a slotted spoon.

SHOPPING LIST

2 tablespoons olive oil

1 tablespoon butter or margarine

1 teaspoon minced garlic

½ red onion, diced

1¼ cup orzo (sold in pasta aisle)

3 teaspoons chicken base (see page: 12) mixed into 3 cups water

3 carrots, chopped small

1 cup broccoli florets, chopped into bite sized pieces

½ cup finely chopped red bell pepper

1 tablespoon parsley flakes

⅓ cup grated or shredded Parmesan cheese

Salt and pepper to taste

Bob's Tips

Though you can't find it in all stores, tricolored orzo pasta makes this lively dish even more vibrant. If orzo isn't readily available or just isn't your cup of tea, try 2 cups of bow-tie pasta in its place—extending the cooking time to 5 minutes under HIGH pressure.

PASTA

MOROCCAN COUSCOUS

THIS RECIPE FOR COUSCOUS—TINY, ALMOST granulated pasta—is a typical Moroccan preparation with chopped dates and cinnamon, adding slight sweetness to this otherwise savory dish. For the best results, keep an eye out for regular uncooked couscous (usually sold in a clear plastic jar), not the instant variety that comes in a box.

1. PLACE oil, onion, bell pepper, and dates in pressure cooker, and heat on HIGH or "BROWN" with the lid off, stirring constantly for 2–3 minutes, until onions are sweating.

2. ADD remaining ingredients. Securely lock on cooker's lid, set cooker to HIGH, and cook 2 minutes.

SHOPPING LIST

2 tablespoons olive oil

½ onion, diced

½ red bell pepper, diced

½ cup chopped dates

2 cups couscous, uncooked

3 cups vegetable broth

1 tablespoon lemon juice

1½ teaspoons ground cinnamon

Salt and pepper to taste

3. PERFORM a quick release to release cooker's pressure, and safely remove lid. Salt and pepper to taste, and serve.

If you like spice, try adding ½ teaspoon cayenne pepper before cooking for a bit of a kick. I like to serve this garnished with chopped pecans or toasted almonds.

PASTA

PENNE ALLA VODKA

THIS PASTA HAS HAD A LITTLE TOO MUCH to drink, and now it's blushing. An American Italian classic, Penne Alla Vodka combines a red and white sauce with a shot of its namesake alcohol for a distinctive flavor that's a knock-out punch guaranteed to leave you punch-drunk.

1. ADD all ingredients, except heavy cream and Parmesan cheese, to cooker. Securely lock on cooker's lid, set cooker to HIGH, and cook 7 minutes.

2. PERFORM a quick release to release cooker's pressure, and safely remove lid.

3. SLOWLY stir in heavy cream and Parmesan cheese, until melted and creamy. Salt and pepper to taste, and serve immediately.

SHOPPING LIST

3 cups penne pasta, uncooked

1½ cups water

1 (24- to 26-ounce) jar marinara sauce

1 (14- to 16-ounce) can diced tomatoes

2 tablespoons butter or margarine

2 teaspoons minced garlic

¼ cup vodka

½ cup heavy cream

¼ cup grated Parmesan cheese

Salt and pepper to taste

Bob's Tips

Skip the vodka, and start off by sautéing ½ cup diced bacon in pressure cooker on HIGH or "BROWN" with the lid off, before step 1 in the recipe for a more family-friendly dish that may just be better than the original!

PASTA

CHEESE TORTELLINI ALFREDO WITH HAM

When you're feeding the whole family, this is a grown-up dish that the kids are guaranteed to love. And with so little prep time, it's something you can literally whip together in only ten minutes…another good thing when feeding a whole family!

1. ADD all Tortellini ingredients to pressure cooker. Securely lock on cooker's lid, set cooker to HIGH, and cook 4 minutes.

2. PERFORM a quick release to release cooker's pressure, and safely remove lid.

3. SLOWLY stir in Dairy ingredients until melted and creamy. Salt to taste, and serve immediately.

Bob's Tips

If the sauce is too thin, add more cream cheese until you get the right consistency; too thick, just add more milk. Go full Italian by replacing the cubed ham with cooked, diced pancetta (Italian bacon), or try ⅔ cup precooked bacon pieces, sold in the salad dressing aisle of your grocery store.

SHOPPING LIST

TORTELLINI

1 (13-ounce) bag dried cheese tortellini (sold in pasta aisle)

1½ cups cubed or diced ham (can buy already cubed in most stores)

2½ cups water

3 tablespoons butter or margarine

½ teaspoon garlic powder

¼ teaspoon ground black pepper

⅛ teaspoon nutmeg

DAIRY

¾ cup grated Parmesan cheese

¾ cup whole milk

4 ounces cream cheese (½ regular-size brick)

Salt to taste

PASTA

BACON TOMATO ROTINI WITH PEAS

THIS CREAMY ROTINI DISH IS FULL OF COLOR and flavor! Put together a salad while the pasta is cooking, and you have a full meal in under 10 minutes for only a fraction of the price that you would spend at one of those big pasta restaurants.

1. ADD rotini, chicken base mixture, water, and butter to pressure cooker. Securely lock on cooker's lid, set cooker to HIGH, and cook 6 minutes.

2. PERFORM a quick release to release cooker's pressure. Safely remove lid, and slowly stir in bacon pieces, Parmesan cheese, and milk.

3. SET cooker to HIGH or "BROWN" with the lid off. Slowly add cornstarch mixture, and simmer 2 minutes after it begins to thicken.

4. STIR in chopped tomatoes, peas, and parsley. Salt and pepper to taste, and serve immediately.

SHOPPING LIST

3 cups rotini pasta

2 teaspoons chicken base (see page: 12) mixed into 2 cups water

1 cup water

2 tablespoons butter or margarine

¾ cup cooked bacon pieces (sold precooked in salad dressing aisle)

½ cup grated Parmesan cheese

1 cup milk

2 tablespoons cornstarch, mixed with 2 tablespoons water

2 tomatoes, chopped

1 cup frozen peas

2 teaspoons parsley flakes

Salt and pepper to taste

PASTA

Bob's Tips

I make this dish with tri-color rotini, but penne pasta can be easily substituted. Mini penne pasta gives the dish a real restaurant-quality presentation.

SAUCES

BOLOGNESE SAUCE

THIS ITALIAN MEAT SAUCE IS SO VERSATILE, you may want to make up two batches and freeze one for a rainy day! Of course, with only an eight-minute cook time you won't get much faster than just making it from scratch! I like this served over petite penne pasta, but when it comes to meat sauce, it's hard to beat the classic comfort combination with spaghetti.

1. POUR olive oil into pressure cooker, and heat on HIGH or "BROWN" with the lid off, until sizzling.

2. ADD onion and garlic, and stir constantly for 1 minute.

3. ADD ground beef and Italian sausage, and cook 2–3 minutes, breaking the meat apart, and browning well.

4. ADD remaining ingredients. Securely lock on cooker's lid, set cooker to HIGH, and cook 8 minutes.

5. LET pressure release naturally 10 minutes before quick releasing remaining pressure and safely removing the lid. Salt and pepper to taste, and serve over your favorite pasta.

SHOPPING LIST

3 tablespoons olive oil

1 large onion, chopped large

1 tablespoon minced garlic

1 pound ground beef

¼ ground Italian sausage, optional

¼ cup cooked bacon pieces (can buy precooked in salad dressing section)

1 (14- to 16-ounce) can diced tomatoes

1 (14- to 16-ounce) can tomato sauce

½ cup dry white wine

1 bay leaf

1 teaspoon Italian seasoning

1 teaspoon parsley flakes

1 teaspoon sugar

Salt and pepper to taste

Bob's Tips For an amazing casserole, preheat oven to 375°, and boil penne pasta on the stove while sauce is cooking in the pressure cooker. Add cooked penne pasta to a casserole dish, and cover with finished Bolognese sauce. Top sauce with 2 cups shredded mozzarella cheese, and bake 15 minutes, until cheese is melted and bubbling. Let cool 5 minutes before serving.

SAUCES

TZATZIKI SAUCE

Tzatziki Sauce is a Greek staple served with gyros or my very own Pork Souvlaki (recipe page: 99). This creamy yogurt sauce with cucumber and dill is a cool and refreshing contrast to any strongly herbed meat, and the perfect "dip" for a warm piece of pita bread. Just don't tell the hummus!

SHOPPING LIST

1 medium cucumber

1 tablespoon minced garlic

1 tablespoon lemon juice

1 tablespoon chopped fresh dill

2 cups plain yogurt

Salt and pepper to taste

1. PEEL cucumber, then slice in half lengthwise. Spoon out the softer, seed-filled portion in the center, and discard. Roughly chop peeled and cleaned cucumber halves.

2. COMBINE all ingredients, except yogurt, in a food processor, and pulse until well blended and cucumber is almost completely grated.

3. SKIM any liquid off the top of yogurt, then combine with cucumber mixture until blended. Salt and pepper to taste, then refrigerate at least 2 hours before serving (for best flavor).

The thicker consistency of Greek yogurt works best for this sauce, so keep an eye out for it in the dairy section of your grocery store. To make your own Greek yogurt, line a colander with 2 coffee filters (one right inside of the other), and place colander over a bowl. Pour regular, plain yogurt into coffee filters, and refrigerate for 4 hours as the water drains out of the yogurt.

SAUCES

PUTTANESCA SAUCE

PUTTANESCA SAUCE, ONCE AN ITALIAN way to utilize leftovers with a little of this, and a little of that, its ingredients have somewhat standardized over time. A strong pasta sauce, most of its flavor comes from anchovy fillets that literally dissolve right into it as it cooks.

1. POUR olive oil into pressure cooker, and heat on HIGH or "BROWN" with the lid off, until sizzling.

2. ADD garlic and anchovies, and stir constantly, until anchovies break apart entirely, almost dissolving.

3. ADD remaining ingredients, except parsley flakes. Securely lock on cooker's lid, set cooker to HIGH, and cook 5 minutes.

SHOPPING LIST

3 tablespoons olive oil

1 tablespoon minced garlic

2 anchovy fillets

1 (32-ounce) can whole tomatoes

¼ cup kalamata olives, pitted and chopped

1 tablespoon capers

¼ cup dry red wine

½ teaspoon crushed red pepper

1 teaspoon dried basil

1 tablespoon parsley flakes

4. LET pressure release naturally 5 minutes before quick releasing remaining pressure. Safely remove the lid, and stir well to break apart tomatoes. Add parsley flakes, and serve over your favorite pasta.

Bob's Tips

If anchovies aren't your thing, try replacing with ¼ cup of diced pancetta (Italian bacon) or prosciutto (Italian ham). They carry their own uniquely strong flavors without anything fishy going on!

SAUCES

PREP TIME	COOK TIME		SERVES	TEMPERATURE
5 MINS	4 MINS		SIXTEEN	LOW

STRAWBERRY SAUCE

THIS SIMPLE STRAWBERRY SAUCE IS A five minute, make-ahead treat that is almost a prerequisite for your next *Vanilla Bean Cheesecake* (recipe page: 191). Whether you'd like to add a homemade touch to store-bought ice cream or make the perfect strawberry shortcake, this sauce is as easy as it gets!

SHOPPING LIST

1 (16-ounce) bag frozen strawberries

1 teaspoon cornstarch

1 cup water

1 cup sugar

¼ teaspoon vanilla extract

1 teaspoon lemon juice

1. CUT open bag of frozen strawberries, and add cornstarch directly into bag. Hold bag closed, and shake to lightly coat strawberries.

2. ADD coated strawberries to pressure cooker, cover with remaining ingredients, and stir.

3. SECURELY lock on cooker's lid, set cooker to LOW, and cook 4 minutes.

4. LET pressure release naturally at least 10 minutes before quick releasing remaining pressure to safely remove lid. Keep your hand away from the steam as you release remaining pressure, as it could spit extremely hot sauce. Serve as a hot sundae topping, or refrigerate at least 2 hours to serve cold.

Though this recipe is easiest, most inexpensive, and quite good with frozen strawberries, fresh are even better. Try substituting with two pints of fresh strawberries, tops removed. If the fresh strawberries are particularly good and sweet, you may want to cut the added sugar down from 1 cup to ¾ cup.

SAUCES

HORSERADISH CREAM

This luxuriously creamy horseradish sauce may bring a tear to your eye... literally. If you like it hot, then this one's for you. Serve with steaks, roast beef, corned beef, or even as a fresh vegetable dip—if you dare!

1. COMBINE all ingredients in mixing bowl or food storage container, and mix until well blended.

2. REFRIGERATE at least 2 hours to unlock the most flavors before serving alongside your favorite dish.

SHOPPING LIST

1 cup reduced-fat sour cream

2 tablespoons horseradish, jarred

1 tablespoon Dijon mustard

¼ teaspoon sugar

Salt and pepper to taste

Bob's Tips

Serve with my recipe for Traditional Corned Beef and Cabbage (recipe page: 41). Or spread on a kaiser roll piled high with thinly carved Perfect Pot Roast (recipe page: 37).

SAUCES

STICK TO YOUR RIBS BBQ SAUCE

THIS NO COOK RECIPE FOR BBQ SAUCE IS my tailor-made secret to pressure cooking sweet and tangy barbecue dishes. It's made extra, extra thick to hold up well when combined with other liquids in pressure cooker recipes, and when basting and re-basting your BBQ sauce just isn't an option.

1. COMBINE all ingredients in mixing bowl, large jar, or food storage container, and mix until well blended.

2. REFRIGERATE overnight to unlock the most flavors before using it to make your favorite pressure cooking barbecue dish.

This sauce is the perfect consistency for my BBQ Brisket (recipe page: 55). It mixes with the beer without turning into water. Try topping a burger, or even meatloaf, with this sauce instead of ketchup to bring a little more flavor to the table!

SHOPPING LIST

2 (6-ounce) cans tomato paste

⅓ cup white vinegar

¼ cup water

3 tablespoons light brown sugar

1 tablespoon molasses

1 tablespoon Dijon mustard

1 teaspoon liquid smoke

½ teaspoon paprika

1 teaspoon garlic powder

1 teaspoon onion powder

½ teaspoon celery salt

¼ teaspoon ground black pepper

Pinch of cinnamon

SAUCES

CRANBERRY SAUCE

THIS FRESH CRANBERRY SAUCE'S TART bite is sure to sweeten up the holidays. You may want to warn the kids, though, because like any real cranberry sauce, the final result is actually a chunky sauce, and not the can-shaped gelatin found in supermarkets.

1. COMBINE all ingredients in pressure cooker, and stir.

2. SECURELY lock on cooker's lid, set cooker to HIGH, and cook 6 minutes.

SHOPPING LIST

12 ounces fresh cranberries (about 3 cups)

1 cup sugar

⅔ cup water

1 teaspoon orange zest

3. LET pressure release naturally 5 minutes before performing a quick release to release remaining pressure and safely removing the lid. Stir sauce, smashing cranberries, until sauce is at your desired consistency. Let sit an additional 5 minutes to firm slightly before serving warm.

Bob's Tips Cranberries literally pop while they cook, so do not be alarmed if it sounds like you're making popcorn! People are pretty accustomed to a cold cranberry sauce these days, which gives you plenty of time to prepare this before Turkey Day. The pectin in the cranberries will thicken the sauce even further after a few hours of refrigeration.

SAUCES

DESSERTS

VANILLA BEAN CHEESECAKE

With three forms of vanilla, it's safe to say that this cheesecake is anything but…vanilla. While simple enough to please classic cheesecake fans, the fresh vanilla bean seeds speckled throughout is only slightly less impressive than the taste!

1. MIX cookie crumbs with butter, and press into bottom of a 7-inch springform pan to form the crust.

2. SLICE vanilla bean lengthwise, and scrape seeds into an electric mixer or food processor. Add cream cheese, sugar, eggs, yogurt, flour, and vanilla extract, and mix on medium speed until very fluffy.

3. SPREAD mixture over crust. Tightly cover pan with aluminum foil.

SHOPPING LIST

1 cup crumbled butter cookies

2 tablespoons butter, melted

1 vanilla bean

2 (8-ounce) packages cream cheese, softened

¾ cup sugar

3 large eggs

½ cup vanilla yogurt

1 tablespoon flour

1 teaspoon vanilla extract

2½ cups water

Whipped cream, to top

4. POUR water into pressure cooker, and place a metal rack on the bottom. Place springform pan on the rack. Securely lock on cooker's lid, set cooker to HIGH, and cook 25 minutes.

5. LET pressure release naturally 10 minutes before performing a quick release to release remaining pressure. Safely remove lid, and let cool in cooker at least 10 minutes before removing pan. Do not attempt to remove the pan while still hot!

6. REFRIGERATE 1 hour, uncovered (blotting any water on top of cake with a paper towel to keep cake dry). Cover with aluminum foil, and refrigerate at least 6 hours before serving; top with whipped cream.

It almost goes without saying that you should try this topped with Strawberry Sauce (recipe page: 185). Or serve it as is, topped with fresh vanilla beans for garnish.

DESSERTS

RUM RAISIN BREAD PUDDING

I LIKE TO TOP THIS OFF WITH A SCOOP OF vanilla ice cream and a drizzle of rum sauce (recipe in my tips below).

1. SPRAY a metal cake or pie pan (small enough to fit into pressure cooker with room around the sides) with nonstick cooking spray, and add bread to pan.

2. ADD water to cooker, and place pan over top. For best results, place pan on top of a metal pressure cooker rack.

3. WHISK remaining ingredients, except whipped cream, in a mixing bowl, then pour over bread. Cover pan with aluminum foil.

4. SECURELY lock on cooker's lid, set cooker to HIGH, and cook 15 minutes.

5. LET pressure release naturally 15 minutes before quick releasing any remaining pressure and safely removing the lid. Let cool in cooker at least 10 minutes before removing pan. Do not attempt to remove the pan while still hot!

6. RUN a knife around edges of pudding, then flip onto a serving dish, tapping the bottom until pudding releases. Serve warm, topped with whipped cream.

SHOPPING LIST

Nonstick cooking spray

4 cups French bread, cut into 1-inch cubes

1½ cups water, for water bath

½ cup raisins

1 cup half-and-half

1 tablespoon butter or margarine, melted

2 large eggs

¼ cup light brown sugar

¼ cup sugar

½ teaspoon cinnamon

½ teaspoon rum extract

⅛ teaspoon nutmeg

Whipped cream, to top

Bob's Tips

To make a quick and easy rum sauce topping: Combine 1 cup sugar, ½ cup milk, 1 teaspoon rum extract, and 1 tablespoon butter in a saucepan, and sauté on the stovetop over medium heat. Thicken with 1 tablespoon cornstarch mixed into 1 tablespoon water, stirring into sauce while simmering.

Prep Time	Cook Time		Serves	Temperature
15 MINS	15 MINS		SIX	HIGH

COCONUT CUSTARD

THIS EXOTIC, YET SIMPLE DESSERT'S COOL flavor and smooth texture are the perfect palate pleasers after a spicy dinner...or after any dinner...or not even after dinner at all. Basically, I just love custard!

1. SPRAY a metal cake or pie pan (small enough to fit into pressure cooker with room around the sides) with nonstick cooking spray.

2. ADD water to cooker, and place pan over top. For best results, place pan on top of a metal pressure cooker rack.

SHOPPING LIST

Nonstick cooking spray

1 cup water, for water bath

2 large eggs

2 large egg yolks

1 (14-ounce) can sweetened condensed milk

¾ cup unsweetened coconut flakes

1 teaspoon vanilla extract

3. MIX remaining ingredients in a mixing bowl until well blended, then pour into pan about 1½ inches high. Depending on pan size, you may have enough for 2 batches. Cover pan with aluminum foil.

4. SECURELY lock on cooker's lid, set cooker to HIGH, and cook 5 minutes.

5. LET pressure release naturally 10 minutes before quick releasing any remaining pressure, and safely removing the lid. Let cool in cooker at least 20 minutes before removing pan. Do not attempt to remove the pan while still hot!

6. REFRIGERATE at least 3 hours before serving. To serve, run a knife around edges of custard, then flip custard onto a serving dish, tapping the bottom until custard releases.

Bob's Tips

Serve topped with fresh mango slices or canned pineapple rings and toasted coconut. Or sauté equal parts dark rum, butter, and sugar in a saucepan for 2–3 minutes for a quick and easy rum sauce.

DESSERTS

CINNAMON APPLES WITH GRANOLA AND ICE CREAM

I SHOULD REALLY CALL THIS RECIPE Instant Apple Cobbler, because three minutes simply must be the fastest any cobbler has seen the light of day. It's a tough call as to whether a cobbler is still a cobbler if the topping isn't cooked in the same dish as the fruit, but I'll tell you what, my taste buds certainly can't tell the difference! Steaming hot cinnamon apples, crunchy topping, and ice cold vanilla ice cream—well, it's as American as Apple COBBLER!

1. Toss sliced apples in a bowl with flour, until evenly coated. Place in pressure cooker, cover with remaining Cinnamon Apples ingredients, and stir.

2. SECURELY lock on cooker's lid, set cooker to HIGH, and cook 3 minutes.

3. PERFORM quick release to release cooker's pressure. Safely remove lid, and let cool 3 minutes.

SHOPPING LIST

CINNAMON APPLES

3 red apples, peeled, cored, and cut into ¾-inch slices

½ cup flour

2 cups water

½ cup sugar

¼ cup light brown sugar

1 tablespoon butter or margarine

2 teaspoons ground cinnamon

1 teaspoon vanilla extract

TOPPING

8 ounces granola clusters or granola cereal

4 scoops vanilla ice cream

4. SPOON apples into 4 individual serving dishes; top with granola and scoop of vanilla ice cream.

Bob's Tips

To crunch up the granola, try baking it on a sheet pan at 350° until it browns, about 5 minutes. You can also prepare these in advance, and keep the individual dishes in the fridge until dessert time, microwaving each on HIGH for 1 minute before topping with the granola and ice cream.

DESSERTS

KEY LIME CHEESECAKE

T HIS TWIST ON CHEESECAKE IS EVERY BIT as refreshing as its inspiration, without veering too far away from the things you love about a traditional, rich cheesecake.

1. MIX vanilla wafer crumbs with butter, and press into bottom of 7-inch springform pan to form crust.

2. MIX cream cheese, Key lime juice, sugar, eggs, yogurt, flour, and vanilla with an electric mixer on medium speed until well blended and fluffy. Pour over crust, and tightly cover pan with aluminum foil.

3. POUR water into pressure cooker, place a metal rack on bottom, then place springform pan on rack. Securely lock on cooker's lid, set cooker to HIGH, and cook 25 minutes.

SHOPPING LIST

1 cup crumbled vanilla wafers

2 tablespoons butter or margarine, softened

2 (8-ounce) packages cream cheese, softened

4 tablespoons Key lime juice

¾ cup sugar

3 large eggs

½ cup plain yogurt

1 tablespoon flour

1 teaspoon vanilla extract

2½ cups water

Whipped cream, to top

1 Key lime, sliced, for garnish

4. LET pressure release naturally 10 minutes before performing a quick release to release remaining pressure. Safely remove lid, and let cool in cooker at least 10 minutes before removing pan. Do not attempt to remove the pan while still hot!

5. REFRIGERATE 1 hour, uncovered (blotting any water on top of cake with a paper towel to keep cake dry), then cover with aluminum foil, and refrigerate an additional minimum of 6 hours before serving topped with whipped cream and fresh lime slices.

It's an absolute must that real Key lime juice be used in this recipe! Real Key lime juice has very little color (don't buy anything that's a bright neon green!), and the flavor is more tart than traditional lime juice.

BANANA NUT BREAD PUDDING

HOW THE PRESSURE COOKER BAKES FRESH, warm banana nut bread, then cubes it, and turns it into bread pudding in just 15 minutes I'll never know!

1. SPRAY a metal cake or pie pan (small enough to fit into pressure cooker with room around the sides) with nonstick cooking spray, then add bread and pecans.

2. ADD water to cooker, and place pan over top. For best results, place pan on top of a metal pressure cooker rack.

3. WHISK remaining ingredients, except whipped cream, in a mixing bowl until well blended; pour over bread. Cover pan with aluminum foil

4. SECURELY lock on cooker's lid, set cooker to HIGH, and cook 15 minutes.

5. LET pressure release naturally 15 minutes before quick releasing any remaining pressure and safely removing the lid. Let cool in cooker at least 10 minutes before removing pan. Do not attempt to remove the pan while still hot!

6. RUN a knife around edges of pudding, then flip onto a serving dish, tapping the bottom until pudding releases. Serve warm with whipped cream.

SHOPPING LIST

Nonstick cooking spray

4 cups honey wheat sandwich bread, lightly toasted, and cut into 1-inch cubes

¼ cup chopped pecans

1½ cups water, for water bath

2 bananas, mashed

1 cup half-and-half

1 tablespoon butter or margarine, melted

2 large eggs

¼ cup light brown sugar

¼ cup sugar

½ teaspoon sugar

1 teaspoon vanilla extract

¼ teaspoon cinnamon

Whipped cream, to top

Bob's Tips

I like to serve this topped with warm caramel sauce. Making caramel sauce is touchy and troublesome. Store-bought sauce is quite adequate, and sold in the sundae topping section.

DESSERTS

WHITE CHOCOLATE RICE PUDDING WITH RASPBERRIES

THIS RICE PUDDING IS UNIQUE AND delicious without deviating too far away from what you know and love about the standard. It's rich, creamy, full of texture, and pleasantly packed with the buttery sweet flavor of white chocolate.

1. PLACE butter and rice in pressure cooker, and stir until rice is coated.

2. COVER with water. Securely lock on cooker's lid, set cooker to HIGH, and cook 6 minutes.

3. PERFORM a quick release to release cooker's pressure. Safely remove lid, and stir in remaining ingredients, except raspberries and garnish.

4. LET cool 10 minutes before stirring again. Serve warm, or cover and refrigerate 2–3 hours to serve chilled.

SHOPPING LIST

1 tablespoon butter or margarine, melted

1 cup Arborio or Calrose rice

2 cups water

½ cup sweetened condensed milk

1 cup milk

⅓ cup white chocolate chips

1 teaspoon vanilla extract

⅛ teaspoon nutmeg

1 pint raspberries

Shaved white chocolate or additional chips, for garnish

5. SERVE topped with fresh raspberries and shaved white chocolate or white chocolate chips.

Bob's Tips

I've found that the consistency of rice pudding is a matter of taste. Once chilled, if the pudding thickens too much, simply thin it down with more milk until you get it where you like it.

DESSERTS

CARAMEL CAPPUCCINO FLAN

THIS MODERN TWIST ON THE CLASSIC Spanish dish is an elegant but simple little pick-me-up after a great meal. Make the "decaffeinated" version of this recipe by removing the instant coffee, and you've got yourself a traditional Caramel Flan.

SHOPPING LIST

½ cup sugar

Nonstick cooking spray

1 cup water, for water bath

2 large eggs

½ (14-ounce) can sweetened condensed milk

12 ounces evaporated milk

2 tablespoons instant coffee

½ teaspoon vanilla extract

1. HEAT sugar in a small nonstick pan on stove over medium heat, stirring occasionally, until a caramel color.

2. SPRAY a metal cake or pie pan (small enough to fit into pressure cooker with room around the sides) with nonstick cooking spray. Pour caramelized sugar into pan, and tilt from side to side to coat the bottom.

3. ADD water to cooker, and place sugared pan over top. For best results, place pan on top of a metal pressure cooker rack.

4. MIX remaining ingredients in a mixing bowl until well blended, then pour into pan, over sugar about 1½ inches high. Depending on pan size, you may have enough for 2 batches. Cover pan with foil. Securely lock on cooker's lid, and set cooker to HIGH for 15 minutes.

5. LET pressure release naturally at least 10 minutes before quick releasing any remaining pressure, and safely removing the lid. Let cool in cooker 20 minutes before removing pan. Do not attempt to remove the pan while still hot!

6. REFRIGERATE at least 3 hours before serving. To serve, run a knife around edges of flan, then flip pan onto a serving dish, tapping the bottom until flan releases.

Bob's Tips

If you do not own a cake or pie pan small enough to fit in your pressure cooker, many grocery stores sell disposable pie tins in a full range of sizes. They make cleanup an ease, but are so flimsy that they don't always allow you to remove the flan for serving in one piece!

DESSERTS

PUMPKIN CHEESECAKE

T HE TASTE OF THIS DESSERT'S FALL FLAVORS will bring all the colors of the season to mind. It's far more decadent than pumpkin pie, but with all of its classic flavor!

1. MIX graham cracker crumbs with butter, and press into bottom of 7-inch springform pan to form crust.

2. MIX cream cheese, pumpkin, sugar, eggs, flour, vanilla, and pumpkin pie spice with an electric mixer on medium speed until mixture is well blended and fluffy.

3. POUR mixture over crust. Tightly cover pan with aluminum foil.

4. POUR water into pressure cooker, and place a metal rack on bottom. Place springform pan on rack.

5. SECURELY lock on cooker's lid, set cooker to HIGH, and cook 25 minutes.

SHOPPING LIST

1 cup graham cracker crumbs

2 tablespoons butter or margarine, softened

2 (8-ounce) packages cream cheese, softened

1 cup canned pumpkin

¾ cup sugar

3 large eggs

1 tablespoon flour

2 teaspoons vanilla extract

1½ teaspoons pumpkin pie spice

2½ cups water

¾ cup chopped pecans, to top

Whipped cream, to top

6. LET pressure release naturally 10 minutes before performing a quick release to release remaining pressure. Safely remove lid, and let cool in cooker at least 10 minutes before removing pan. Do not attempt to remove the pan while still hot!

7. REFRIGERATE 1 hour, uncovered (blotting any water on top of cake with a paper towel to keep cake dry). Cover with foil, and refrigerate an additional 6 hours. Top entire cake with a layer of chopped pecans, and dabs of whipped cream before serving.

 Bob's Tips Unsweetened, canned pumpkin works best in this recipe, not pumpkin pie filling…but pumpkin pie filling would work in a pinch.

DESSERTS

GINGERSNAP PEAR BREAD PUDDING

Gingersnap cookies make this bread pudding anything but day old bread! Add thinly sliced pears, and you've got a uniquely satisfying combination. I serve it warm, topped with butter pecan ice cream.

1. SPRAY a metal cake or pie pan (small enough to fit into pressure cooker with room around the sides) with nonstick cooking spray, then add bread and cookie crumbs to pan. Cover with sliced pears.

2. ADD water to cooker, and place pan over top. For best results, place pan on top of a metal pressure cooker rack.

3. WHISK remaining ingredients, except whipped cream, in a mixing bowl until well blended, then pour over bread. Cover pan with aluminum foil.

4. SECURELY lock on cooker's lid, set cooker to HIGH, and cook 15 minutes.

SHOPPING LIST

Nonstick cooking spray

3 cups French bread, cut into 1-inch cubes

1½ cups crumbled gingersnap cookies

1½ cups water, for water bath

2 pears, peeled and sliced ⅙ inch thick

1 cup half-and-half

1 tablespoon butter or margarine, melted

2 large eggs

¼ cup light brown sugar

¼ cup sugar

½ teaspoon allspice

½ teaspoon vanilla extract

⅛ teaspoon nutmeg

Whipped cream, to top

5. LET pressure release naturally 15 minutes before quick releasing any remaining pressure and safely removing the lid. Let cool in cooker 10 minutes before removing pan. Do not attempt to remove the pan while still hot!

6. RUN a knife around edges of pudding, then flip onto a serving dish, tapping the bottom until pudding releases. Serve warm, topped with whipped cream.

Bob's Tips This recipe is even better when reheated the next day. The flavors have all night to mingle, and mingle they do!

DESSERTS

LEMON PUDDING WITH COOKIE CRUMB SWIRL

THERE'S SOMETHING FULFILLING ABOUT making pudding from scratch. You just can't beat the fresh (and tart!) lemon taste of this recipe. Top it with the crumbled vanilla wafer cookies for the perfect presentation.

1. IN a mixing bowl, combine egg yolks, flour, butter, lemon zest, lemon juice, lemon extract, milk, and sugar

2. USING an electric mixer, beat egg whites until soft peaks form.

3. FOLD egg whites into first mixture, then pour into a cake or pie pan (small enough to fit into pressure cooker with room around the sides). Cover pan with aluminum foil, sealing edges well.

SHOPPING LIST

2 large eggs, yolks and whites separated

2 tablespoons flour

1 tablespoon butter

Zest of 1 lemon

2 tablespoons lemon juice

½ teaspoon lemon extract

⅔ cup milk

½ cup sugar

2 cups water, for water bath

8 vanilla wafers, crumbled

4. ADD water to cooker, and place pan over top. For best results, place pan on top of a metal pressure cooker rack. Securely lock on cooker's lid, set cooker to HIGH, and cook 7 minutes.

5. LET pressure release naturally 10 minutes before quick releasing any remaining pressure, and safely removing the lid. Let cool in cooker 10 minutes before removing pan. Do not attempt to remove the pan while still hot!

6. COVER, and refrigerate 2–3 hours before serving. Serve topped with a swirl of vanilla wafer cookie crumbs.

The cookie crumb swirl is a wonderful presentation, but you may want to keep a handful of whole vanilla wafers on hand to dip into the pudding. Once you get a taste of the crumbs you may want something with a little more substance!

Recipe Index

BOB WARDEN

IN THE TWENTY-FIVE YEARS BOB WARDEN has been appearing as a guest cooking expert on home shopping networks, he has helped develop hundreds of kitchen products. With great expertise in pressure cookery, he has sold over a million electric pressure cookers while on the air! He is also the author of ten cookbooks, and co-author with Gwen McKee of the *Best of the Best Cook's Essentials Cookbook*. Bob has written *Bob Warden's Slow Food Fast* and *Great Food Fast* especially for today's home chef who is looking for quick and easy ways to pressure cook great, everyday meals, without sacrificing quality or flavor.